THE CHALLENGE OF PREACHING

A GIFT TO YOU FROM
LANGHAM PARTNERSHIP

*May this book draw you
near to Jesus Christ and equip you
to share His love with others.*

www.langham.org

D0721754

THE CHALLENGE OF PREACHING

John Stott

Abridged and updated by

Greg Scharf

PREACHING RESOURCES

© 2013 by John Stott and Greg Scharf

Published 2013 by Langham Preaching Resources
an imprint of Langham Creative Projects

Langham Partnership

PO Box 296, Carlisle, Cumbria, CA3 9WZ

www.langham.org

Based on *I Believe in Preaching*, first published in 1982 in the U.K. by Hodder and Stoughton, London.

Abridged and updated by Greg Scharf with the approval of John Stott and under licence from Hodder and Stoughton.

ISBNs:
978-1-907713-11-8 print
978-1-907713-13-2 Mobi
978-1-907713-12-5 ePub

British Library Cataloguing in Publication Data

Stott, John R. W.
    The challenge of preaching. -- Abridged and updated ed.
    1. Preaching.
    I. Title II. Scharf, Greg. III. Stott, John R. W. I believe
    in preaching.
    251-dc22

Cover design: Luz Design www.projectluz.com

Book design: To a Tee Ltd, www.2at.com

CONTENTS

LANGHAM PREACHING RESOURCES

In a remarkable sentence written to the Thessalonians, Paul gave us a clear statement about the dynamic impact of God's word.

> *And we also thank God continually because, when you received the word of God, which you heard from us, you accepted it not as a human word, but as it actually is, the word of God, which is indeed at work in you who believe.* (1 Thess 2:13)

He makes the point emphatically. The message is not a human word but is the authoritative word *of God*. And this word is powerful: it is 'at work in you'. And it had its impact in the lives of the Thessalonian believers because they not only heard that word but also accepted it, welcoming it in like a friend.

All preaching must be shaped by the conviction that scripture is authoritative, precisely because it comes from God himself. And all preachers must be persuaded of the fact that God's word is powerful, at work to achieve God's purposes in the lives of individuals and Christian communities. And all listeners must welcome that word, accepting it with faith, allowing it to change them as it did the Thessalonians, who 'turned to God from idols to serve the living and true God' (1 Thess 1:9).

Preachers and teachers who are committed to proclaiming God's word need to be supported, and this is what *Langham Partnership* seeks to do, in fellowship with the global church, through the programmes of Langham Literature, Langham Scholars and Langham Preaching.

Launched by Dr John Stott some 35 years ago, Langham is founded on a strong commitment to the authority of the Bible and the importance of faithful, relevant and clear Bible preaching. The basic conviction that shapes the work is *that God wants his church to grow up, that God's church grows through God's word, and that God's word comes to us mostly through effective preaching.*

Strengthening biblical preaching is the foundation for growing strong and effective churches. So Langham Preaching works with national leaders to nurture indigenous national preaching movements for pastors and lay preachers all around the world. Together we provide practical support for preachers by organising training seminars, encouraging preachers groups, providing resources and building national movements committed to biblical preaching.

Now we are seeking to add to that support by providing *Langham Preaching Resources*. These are accessible materials for pastors and preachers, particularly those involved in the preaching movements that are now emerging in every region of the world, and increasingly they are being made available in several languages.

Our prayer is that these resources will serve to strengthen biblical preaching. They are written and distributed with the same prayer Paul made as he wrote to those Thessalonian believers, who welcomed God's word so enthusiastically.

Pray for us, that the message of the Lord may spread rapidly and be honoured, just as it was with you. (2 Thess 3:1)

Jonathan Lamb
Director, Langham Preaching

For more information about the three Langham programmes, please visit our web site, **www.langham.org**

FOREWORD

In 1959 the young John Stott was appointed rector of All Souls Church, Langham Place, in the heart of London. There his regular exposition of the Bible as a pastor and teacher became so influential that over time his ministry has spread to every corner of the globe. He has become known as a tireless advocate and friend of the church in Africa, Asia and Latin America, where the church has been growing so rapidly under such extraordinary pressure. The memory of 'uncle John' is held in deep affection by church leaders and church members across those continents.

The various programmes John Stott founded to serve the global church family have been amalgamated under the name of *Langham Partnership*, which seeks to help the church grow to maturity by equipping a new generation of preachers and teachers. It is motivated to fulfil John Stott's vision of seeing every pulpit worldwide occupied by preachers who are committed to the faithful and relevant exposition of the Bible.

John Stott's preaching and writing have always been characterised by three things: faithfulness to the Bible as the Word of God, relevance to the contemporary world in which we live, and remarkable clarity of expression. All of these qualities are evident in this volume, which is an abridged and updated edition of his earlier work, *I Believe in Preaching* (published in the USA as *Between Two Worlds*). I would like to express our warm thanks to Dr Greg Scharf for his work in providing what will become an invaluable resource to those involved in the Langham Preaching movements around the world.

As this book makes clear, preaching is not only a matter of technique. It is vitally connected to the integrity and character of the preacher. In the case of John Stott, countless people around the world can testify to the godly influence and deep encouragement he has brought to their Christian lives and their Christian communities. His biographer, Timothy Dudley-Smith has this to say:

> *To those who know and meet him, respect and affection go hand in hand. The world figure is lost in personal friendship, disarming interest, unfeigned humility – and a dash of mischievous humour and charm. ... He thinks of himself, as all Christians should but few of us achieve, as simply a beloved child of a heavenly Father, an unworthy servant of his friend and master Jesus Christ, a sinner saved by grace, for the glory and praise of God.*

It is a joy to see *The Challenge of Preaching* made available to a new generation of pastors and preachers around the world. May it stimulate every reader to be more committed to the task of bridge-building - sustaining our faithfulness to scripture alongside our commitment to proclaim its truth with conviction and relevance to our own generation.

Jonathan Lamb
Director, Langham Preaching
Oxford, May 2013

PREFACE

Preaching sank to a low ebb in the last half of the twentieth century. Has it recovered at all? That question is difficult to answer because we do not yet have the benefit of a long-term perspective. What can be said is that two contradictory trends have emerged, both of which have positive and negative implications.

First, preaching has been democratized. Almost anyone can preach, regardless of whether they are ordained. This is not altogether a bad thing. Lay preaching can be used by the Lord to build his church, and we could wish with Moses that all God's people were prophets (Num 11:29). Unfortunately, however, it seems that some preachers' only qualification for ministry is their ability to attract large crowds and donations, and not their commitment to truth and holiness. This trend has been most noticeable among advocates of prosperity teaching, who promise health and wealth in Jesus' name. This distortion of the gospel is proving very popular among those whose social and economic prospects are bleak.

But while preaching is being democratized, it is simultaneously becoming increasingly elitist. Gifted preachers are now able to broadcast their message and preside over multi-site churches where the sermon is presented on video screens. Many such preachers are orthodox, kingdom-minded, and holy, and their impact for good is significant. They can reach out to churches that formerly did not offer solid biblically-based teaching. However, the distance between these preachers and their hearers may undermine the biblical requirement that overseers be an example (1 Tim 3:1–4:16) and that shepherds know their sheep (John 10:1–14). These requirements have always been difficult to fulfil in large churches.

A more subtle danger is that young preachers compare themselves with these exceptional preachers and wrongly conclude that they do not have preaching gifts. Beginners may try to imitate them in superficial ways, rather than working to develop the gifts God has given them. They may also be less likely to be given preaching opportunities as church leaders will be reluctant to use inexperienced preachers when congregations have grown accustomed to excellent preaching.

This book sets out to encourage preachers by reminding them of the importance of their calling; to exhort them to spend time in careful and prayerful sermon preparation; and to remind them of the personal qualities that must characterize every faithful preacher of God's word. When you have finished it, may you too be moved to pray the words that John Stott often prayed before preaching:

> Heavenly Father, we bow in your presence.
> May your word be our rule,
> Your Spirit our teacher,
> And your greater glory our supreme concern
> Through Jesus Christ our Lord.

ACKNOWLEDGEMENTS

I am very grateful to John Stott for the immeasurable impact he has had on my life, preaching, and opportunities for ministry. He was my preaching teacher for one quarter at Trinity Evangelical Divinity School, where I now teach. He was my mentor and example at All Souls, Langham Place, where I was a pastoral intern and staff member. He was the pastor who preached at my wedding. He led a reading group I attended in London. He remains my friend and inspiration. I currently chair the United States partner of the Langham Partnership International of which he is the founder. So my gratitude goes well beyond my thanks that he originally wrote this book.

But I am especially grateful that he did write it. As I worked, with his encouragement and blessing, on this abridgement and revision of his original book, I realized that his impact on my own preaching was far greater than I had recalled. The concepts had so made their way into my bloodstream that I assumed many of them were my own!

I am also grateful to Isobel Stevenson who skilfully edited what I sent her to preserve John Stott's voice while making room for the updates and adjustments that needed to be included. Several esteemed colleagues from the Evangelical Homiletics Society made suggestions that greatly helped my thinking. Many prayer partners contributed significantly though indirectly, as did my favourite prayer partner and encourager, my wife Ruth. To all these, and many others who played crucial parts, I am grateful. I thank God for giving me the strength and opportunity to see this project through to completion and trust that he will use it for his glory.

Greg Scharf
Trinity Evangelical Divinity School, Deerfield, Illinois
January 2011

1

CHALLENGES TO PREACHING

Preaching is indispensible to Christianity because Christianity is based on the truth that God chose to use words to reveal himself to humanity. First, he spoke through his prophets, interpreting his actions in the history of Israel and instructing them to convey his message to his people in speech and writing. Then he spoke in his Son when "the Word became flesh" (John 1:14) and through his Son's words, spoken either directly or through his apostles. Thirdly, he speaks by his Spirit through his servants who preach in his name (Luke 24:47–49). The word of God is thus scriptural, incarnate and contemporary. This point is fundamental to Christianity.

God's speech makes our speech necessary. We are called to pass on the message we have heard to others. We must speak what he has spoken or, in other words, we must preach.

This emphasis of preaching is unique to Christianity. While every religion has its teachers, many of whom teach with authority and charisma, they are all essentially expounding ancient traditions and ethics. Only Christian preachers claim to be heralds proclaiming good news from God and dare to think of themselves as ambassadors or representatives speaking "the very words of God" (1 Pet 4:11).

The importance of preaching has been recognized throughout church history (see Appendix 1). Yet we are told by some that the day of preaching is over and that preaching is a dying art and an outmoded form of communication. These lies have silenced and demoralized preachers. So it is worth our while to look at three contemporary trends that challenge our belief in preaching. They are a general hostility to all authority, the electronic revolution, and a loss of confidence in the gospel.

Hostility to Authority

Ever since the Fall, people have been "hostile to God" and unwilling (even unable!) to "submit to God's law" (Rom 8:7). This basic fact about the human condition has shown itself in a thousand ugly ways. Today, however, this attitude is particularly pronounced and all accepted authorities (family, school, university, state, church, pope, Bible, God) are being challenged worldwide. Some of this rebellion is justified, for it is a responsible and mature protest against authoritarianism and dehumanization in politics, business, education, religion and other areas of society. But Christians must be careful to distinguish between true and false authority; between the tyranny which crushes humanity and the rational, benevolent authority under which we find our authentic human freedom.

As people have won greater freedom from institutions, the target for hostility has shifted to ideas. No idea is unchallenged. It is assumed that everyone has a right to their own opinions, which may not be challenged by anyone, let alone a preacher. Some have even gone so far as to describe sermons as acts of violence against listeners. They question the right of preachers to stand before others, claiming to speak for God.

These attitudes have led some to argue that instead of regarding the congregation as a flock to be fed, a preacher should see them as customers and use the sermon to help them solve their spiritual problems.[1] This type of consumer-oriented preaching dominates North American pulpits and has been exported around the world. The pew now sets the agenda for the pulpit. The sermon's starting point is usually a problem for which the Bible (or some other source) provides a solution. Audience analysis (knowing our listeners) – though vital – now often displaces the careful study of the Bible.

The practice of letting listeners set the agenda for preaching has been reinforced by the widely-held view that there is no objective truth; everything is subjective. Something only becomes true if it resonates with me. This means that the final say about what a passage means rests on individuals whose personal stories resonate with it. If what is said does not fit with the experience of an individual or a community, it is rejected. This attitude undermines the authority of the biblical text. Final authority no longer rests with Scripture but with those reading or hearing it. No wonder so many listeners resist submitting to biblical sermons! They have come to believe that they are the reason sermons are preached and that their experiences – personal and communal – take primacy over the Bible and its claims.

Unfortunately, preachers often reinforce these assumptions by designing sermons and worship services that exalt the listener at the expense of Scripture. Although he was writing in 1950, Cranfield's words still ring true today:

> It is a pathetic feature of contemporary church life that there are still plenty in the pews who clamour for shorter and lighter sermons and bright and easy services and not a few in the pulpits prepared to pander to popular taste. There's a vicious circle: superficial congregations make superficial pastors, and superficial pastors make superficial congregations.[2]

Should we allow ourselves to be stampeded into abandoning preaching? Or should we merely become more dogmatic, repeating our beliefs and statements in an ever-louder voice? Neither of those approaches is effective. So how should we react to this trend?

First, we need to remember the Christian understanding of *human nature*. We were created by God to be morally responsible and free. We cannot therefore accept either licence (which denies responsibility) or slavery (which denies freedom). The mind is free only under the authority of truth, and the will under the authority of righteousness.

Secondly, we need to remember the *doctrine of revelation*. Our beliefs are not something we invented. They were revealed by God. We can thus proclaim the gospel with quiet confidence as good news from God.

Thirdly, we need to remember that our *authority* to preach does not come from our appointment as preachers, nor from the church that ordained us, but from the word of God. If we make this clear, people should be willing to hear, particularly if we show that we ourselves desire to live under biblical authority. One way of doing this is to avoid the introductory formula, "Thus says the Lord", for we do not have the authority of the inspired Old Testament prophets. Nor should we use our Lord's formula "I tell you" (Matt 5:22, 28, 32 etc.), as though we have the authority of Jesus Christ or his apostles. Rather, we should use the words "we" and "us" to indicate that we preach nothing to others that we do not preach to ourselves. Authority and humility are not mutually exclusive.

Fourthly, we need to remember the *relevance of the gospel*. When we present the gospel in a way that shows that it is reasonable and relevant, it carries its own authority and authenticates itself.

Fifthly, we need to remember that a true sermon is *not a monologue*. True preaching is always a dialogue. This does not mean that it involves a debate between two preachers or heckling from the listeners (even though that might enliven the proceedings!). Rather, it involves a silent dialogue between the preacher and the hearers. The preacher should provoke questions in their minds, and then proceed to answer them. The answer should raise further questions, which should also be addressed.

One of the greatest gifts a preacher needs is a sensitive understanding of people and their problems so as to be able to anticipate their reactions. We should not preach on the providence of God who "in all things ... works for the good of those who love him" (Rom 8:28) without showing an awareness of evil and pain. We should not preach on marriage and forget the single people in the congregation, or on Christian joy and forget the sorrows and tragedies some will be experiencing. We cannot expound Christ's promise to answer prayer without remembering that some prayers remain unanswered, or his command not to be anxious without acknowledging that people have good reasons for anxiety. To anticipate people's objections is to cover our flanks against counter-attack.

This type of dialogue between speaker and listeners is often evident in Scripture (e.g. Mal 1:12; 2:17; 3:8). Jesus used it (Luke 10:36; John 13:12), and so did the Apostle Paul (Rom 3:1–6.). We also find it in the preaching of men like Martin Luther and Billy Graham. What we need is the ability to

> out-do the Communist technique of "double-think" and do a Christian "quadruple-think". "Quadruple-thinking" is thinking out what I have to say, then thinking out how the other man will understand what I say, and then re-thinking what I have to say, so that, when I say it, he will think what I am thinking! ... "Quadruple-thinking" involves mental pain and great spiritual sensitivity.[3]

Painful as it is, this approach lessens the offence that authoritative preaching would otherwise give.

The Electronic Age

The past fifty years have seen radical changes in methods of communication, and these have had a profound effect on the church. The effects are felt worldwide, even in locations where electronic media have not yet penetrated deeply.

One set of changes affect those to whom we preach. In the electronic age, people have become *physically lazy* and question why they need to go out to church when they can worship at home by watching a service on the television or on the Web. They have become *intellectually uncritical*, wanting to be entertained, rather than made to think. People have also become *emotionally insensitive*. We witness the horrors of war, famine and poverty, but have become skilled in emotional self-defence, distancing ourselves from others' pain. And we have become *psychologically confused*. We find it difficult to switch from the unreal, crafted world of cyberspace to the real world where we can hear and worship God. Finally people have become *morally disordered*. We have been conned into thinking that the type of behaviour we see on the screen is acceptable, and that "everybody does it".

The electronic age also affects us as preachers. Satellite technology has allowed preachers to broadcast globally, and such broadcasts are too easily taken as representing the ideal for which all preachers should strive. We may find ourselves attempting to copy famous preachers without regard to how their techniques and style suit our own personalities, situations and gifts. Or we may decide to preach a sermon we downloaded from the Web, or ask the congregation to watch a sermon by a famous preacher projected on a screen. All of these things can break the communication that should exist between the preacher and the congregation. A sermon preached elsewhere is not addressed to this particular group of listeners, for the preacher cannot see them and observe and react to their responses.

Our faith in the importance of preaching may also be shaken by the visual input of television. Public speaking in the West no longer predominantly features a speaker addressing a crowd from a lectern or pulpit. Instead we see talk-show hosts roaming a television studio and newsreaders seated behind a desk, apparently looking at us – but actually reading from a Teleprompter. The image of the newsreader alternates with video clips illustrating the events being reported. What we hear are sound bites, which may be memorable but which just as often cater to superficiality. A sermon may feel like a very old-fashioned form of communication.

Those who lack access to advanced technology may become discouraged, thinking that without these tools they cannot preach adequately. Visiting preachers using laptops and PowerPoint presentations may unthinkingly convey that this is standard practice. Humble preachers from remote locations receive an unintended and false message: electronic devices are needed for effective preaching.

How shall we respond to this avalanche of technological advances?

First, let us thank our sovereign Creator for giving us the ability to make tools that can take his word to all nations. In the early church, his word was spread when persecution scattered believers, who "preached the word wherever they went" (Acts 8:1–4). Now radio, television and the Web can be used to spread the good news in regions that cannot easily be reached in other ways.

Secondly, we must pray for wisdom and discernment in the use of the tools that are available to us. The fact that they exist does not mean that we must use them. Paul's words to Timothy also apply to those of us who are rich in technology:

> Command those who are rich in this present world not to be arrogant nor to put their hope in wealth, which is so uncertain, but to put their hope in God, who richly provides us with everything for our enjoyment. Command them to do good, to be rich in good deeds, and to be generous and willing to share. In this way they will lay up treasure for themselves as a firm foundation for the coming age, so that they may take hold of the life that is truly life. (1 Tim 6:17–19)

We must trust God, not our computers, projectors and amplifiers (all of which can crash or lead us into temptation). We should thank God for technology, but not rely on it, and we must be willing to share our tools and our learning, looking to God for real treasure and life.

Thirdly, our use of technology as an aid to preaching must not violate or compromise what Scripture teaches. For instance, hearing God's word should always lead to heeding God's word. Such obedience opens the door to a growing knowledge of God (Col 1:10). So we must avoid using tools merely to make concepts from the Bible easier to grasp; they must also move us towards the faith that leads to obedience (Rom 1:5; 16:26).

God himself supplies the best visual aids. He wants the pastor to be a visual aid to the congregation (Titus 2:7; 1 Tim 4:12). He also wants the congregation to be a visual aid to the watching world, indeed to the whole universe (Matt 5:16; Eph 3:10–11). Virtual images projected on screens are no substitute for real people and loving communities. In a dehumanized society, the fellowship of the local church becomes increasingly important as members meet and talk and listen to one another in person. The best transformational learning (learning that fosters faith and increases obedience to God) happens in community.

Although it is good to seek God's face individually (2 Cor 4:6), isolated believers may not always get the whole picture. We need to hear what others in the body of Christ have to say. Paul's prayer for the church (Eph 3:14–21) underscores this corporate dimension:

> For this reason I kneel before the Father, from whom every family in heaven and on earth derives its name. I pray that out of his glorious riches he may strengthen you [plural] with power through his Spirit in your inner being, so that Christ may dwell in your hearts through faith. And I pray that you, being rooted and established in love, may have power, together with all the Lord's people, to grasp how wide and long and high and deep is the love of Christ, and to know this love that surpasses knowledge – that you may be filled to the measure of all the fullness of God.

Finally, it is important to remember that preaching and worship cannot be divorced. The fact that they are so often separated today accounts for the low level of much contemporary worship. All worship is an intelligent and loving response to the revelation of God. Our worship is poor because our knowledge of God is poor; our knowledge of God is poor because our preaching is poor. But when the word of God is expounded in all its fullness, and the congregation begins to glimpse the glory of the living God, they bow down in solemn awe. It is preaching which accomplishes this. That is why preaching is unique and irreplaceable.

But if our preaching is dull, drab, dowdy, slow or monotonous, we cannot compete in today's world. We have to make our presentation of the truth attractive through variety, colour, illustration, humour and fast-flowing movement.

The Church's Loss of Confidence in the Gospel

To preach means to assume the role of a herald or town crier and to publically proclaim a message. This presupposes that we have something to say. Without a clear and confident message, preaching is impossible. Yet this is what the church seems to lack nowadays.

There is no chance of a recovery of preaching without a prior recovery of conviction. We need to regain our confidence in the truth, relevance and power of the gospel so that we can say with Paul,

> I am so eager to preach the gospel also to you … I am not ashamed of the gospel, because it is the power of God that brings salvation to everyone who believes: first to the Jew, then to the Gentile. (Rom 1:14–16)

We need to get excited about this again. The gospel is good news from God!

The first step in recovering our Christian confidence involves being able to distinguish between assurance, conviction, presumption and bigotry. Conviction and assurance indicate that one is convinced by adequate evidence or argument that something is true. Presumption is a premature assumption of a truth, a confidence resting on inadequate or unexamined foundations. Bigotry is both blind and obstinate; bigots close their eyes to the data and cling to untested and unproven opinions. Presumption and bigotry are incompatible with any serious concern for truth and with worship of the God of truth.

Some degree of Christian conviction and assurance is reasonable. Christianity is grounded in good historical evidence, namely the witness of the writers of the New Testament. The verbs "to know" and "believe" and "be persuaded" are liberally sprinkled throughout the

New Testament. Faith and confidence are regarded as normal in the Christian experience. Indeed, the apostles and evangelists often tell their readers that the purpose of what they are writing is "that you may know" or "that you may believe" (Luke 1:1–4; John 20:31; 1 John 5:13). "Full assurance" and "conviction" are meant to characterize our approach to God in prayer and our proclamation of Christ to the world (Heb 10:22; 1 Thess 1:5). A Christian asks questions, probes problems, confesses ignorance, feels perplexity, but does so within the context of a profound and growing confidence in the reality of God and of his Christ.

We need, secondly, to recognize that the questions others ask about our faith are real and important. They cannot be thoughtlessly dismissed, but must be carefully faced and answered. We may not agree with all the suggested answers, but we have no quarrel with the questions.

Thirdly, we need to encourage Christian scholars as they seek answers to tough questions. This can be lonely work. They need our prayers and fellowship as they wrestle with the tension between openness to new ideas and commitment to Christ. They need to be encouraged to accept some measure of accountability to one another and responsibility for one another in the body of Christ.

Finally, we need to pray more persistently and expectantly for grace from the Holy Spirit of truth. Christian understanding is not possible without his enlightenment, nor is Christian assurance possible without his witness. Honest enquiry and supportive fellowship are crucial, but ultimately only God can convince us about God. Our greatest need, as the Reformers kept insisting, is the testimony of the Holy Spirit. Christians believe that the living God is the Lord of history. We should ask him to push back the forces of unbelief and thank him for what he is doing already around the world.

We have considered three challenges to preaching today. Distrust of authority makes people unwilling to listen. Electronic advances have changed the expectations of both listeners and preachers. The atmosphere of doubt makes many preachers too tentative. But it is time to remember that attack is the best form of defence.

2

THEOLOGICAL FOUNDATIONS FOR PREACHING

The secret of preaching is not mastering certain techniques but being mastered by certain convictions. In other words, theology is more important than methodology. Certainly, there are principles of preaching to be learned and skills to be developed, but it is easy to put too much confidence in these. Technique can only make us orators; if we want to be preachers, theology is what we need. If our theology is right, then we have all the basic insights we need into what we ought to be doing, and all the incentives we need to encourage us to do it faithfully.

True Christian preaching (that is, biblical or "expository" preaching) is extremely rare in today's church. Thoughtful people in many countries are asking for it, but cannot find it. Why is this? The major reason must be a lack of conviction about its importance. So my task in this chapter is to try to convince my readers of the indispensable necessity, for the glory of God and the good of the church, of conscientious biblical preaching.

Let us consider five sets of theological convictions that support the importance of biblical preaching. Any one of these should convince us; the five together leave us without excuse.

Convictions about God

The kind of God we believe in determines the kind of sermons we preach. Three characteristics of God are particularly relevant.

First, *God is light.* "This is the message we have heard from him and declare to you: God is light and in him there is no darkness at all" (1 John 1:5). In John's writing "light" frequently represents truth, as when Jesus claimed to be "the light of the world" (John 8:12). God is not secretive. He delights to make himself known. Just as it is the nature of light to shine, so it is the nature of God to reveal himself. The chief reason why people do not know God is not because he hides from them but because they hide from him. Every preacher needs to take encouragement from the fact that God is light and longs to shine his light into the listeners' darkness (2 Cor 4:4–6).

Secondly, *God has acted* and has revealed himself through his actions. He has shown his power and deity in creation, and heaven and earth display his glory (Ps 19:1; Isa 6:3; Rom 1:19, 20). But God has revealed even more of himself in redemption. When humankind rebelled against him, he did not destroy us but instead planned a rescue mission. He brought Abraham out of Ur, the Israelite slaves out of Egypt, and the exiles home from Babylon. Each of these great acts of liberation led to the making or renewing of the covenant whereby Yahweh made them his people and pledged himself to be their God. The New Testament focuses on another redemption and a new covenant that is described as "better", "more glorious" and "eternal" (Heb 7:22; 8:6; 9:14–23; 13:20; 2 Cor 3:4–11). This came about through God's mightiest acts, namely the birth, death and resurrection of his Son, Jesus Christ. So the God of the Bible is a God of liberating activity, coming to the rescue of oppressed humanity and revealing his grace or generosity.

Thirdly, *God has spoken.* God has actually communicated with his people by speech. The Old Testament prophets often stated that "the word of the Lord" came to them. Unlike idols which "have mouths, but cannot speak" (Ps 115:5), the living God spoke to his people (Isa 40:5; 55:11). He did so in order to explain what he was doing. He brought Abraham out of Ur and then he spoke to him about his purpose and gave him the covenant of promise. He led the people of Israel out of slavery in Egypt and appointed Moses to teach them why he was doing this. He brought his people out of exile in Babylon and used his prophets to explain why his judgment had fallen upon them, under what conditions he would restore them, and the kind of people he wanted them to be.

He sent his Son to become man, to live and serve on earth, to die, to rise, to reign and to pour out his Spirit. Then he chose and equipped the apostles to see his works, hear his words, and bear witness to what they had seen and heard.

There are those who emphasize the historical activity of God but deny that he has spoken. They argue that God revealed himself in deeds, not words. They insist that the redemption is the only revelation. But this is false. Scripture affirms that God has spoken both through historical deeds and through explanatory words, and that the two belong together. Even the climax of God's self-revelation, when the Word became flesh, would have remained incomprehensible if Christ had not spoken and his apostles had not recorded and interpreted his words.

This is the foundation on which all Christian preaching rests. How would we dare to speak if God had not spoken? By ourselves we have nothing to say. To speak without the assurance that we bring a message from God would be arrogant and foolish. But if we are convinced that God is light and wants to be known, that God has acted to make himself known, that God has spoken and explained his actions, then we must speak. If we are not sure of this, we would do better to keep our mouths shut. But once we are persuaded that God has spoken, we cannot and must not be silent.

Convictions about Scripture

Our understanding of God naturally influences our beliefs about the Scriptures. After all, *Scripture is God's word written*. What would have been the point of God's revelation of himself in Israel and his unique revelation in Jesus Christ if it had been forgotten over the centuries? So God made provision for a reliable record of his deeds and words to be preserved for all people in all ages and all places. Although 2000 years now separate us from Jesus' deeds and words, we can still know and reach him through the Bible as the Holy Spirit witnesses to him in its pages. Only in the Bible can we find the full facts of Jesus' birth and life, his words and works, his death and resurrection, and God's own authoritative explanation of them. Here and here only is God's own interpretation of his redeeming action.

What is the relevance of this to our preaching? Our responsibility as preachers is not primarily to give our twenty-first century testimony to Jesus, but rather to relay to our listeners God's own authoritative witness to Christ through the eyewitness accounts of the apostles. It is true that the New Testament documents were written in first-century Christian communities. It is true that the needs of these communities to some extent influenced what was preserved. It is true that each writer selected and presented his material according to his particular purposes. Yet neither the churches nor the writers invented or distorted their message. Nor does its authority rest on them or on their faith. None of the apostles or evangelists wrote in the name of a church or churches. Instead, they challenged the churches in the name and with the authority of Jesus Christ. Later, when it was being decided which books should be included in the New Testament, the church did not give authority to the chosen books. The church simply recognized that the chosen books already had authority because they contained the inspired teaching of the apostles.

We who recognize the authority of Scripture should be the most conscientious preachers. If the Scriptures were just a collection of human ideas reflecting the faith of the earliest Christians – with an occasional flash of divine inspiration – then a casual attitude would be excusable. However, in Scripture we are handling the very words of the living God, "not ... taught us by human wisdom but ... taught by the Spirit" (1 Cor 2:13). Nothing should be too much trouble as we study and expound them.

We also need to remember to reflect both the saving acts and the written words of God in our preaching. Some preachers love to speak about the mighty acts of God but present only their own interpretation of them. Others try to stick to God's word but are dull because they have lost the excitement of what God has done in Christ. The true preacher enthusiastically and faithfully conveys both. When God spoke, his normal method was not to shout in an audible voice out of a clear blue sky. Inspiration is not dictation. Instead he put his word into human minds and human mouths in such a way that their thoughts and words were simultaneously and completely theirs as well as his. Inspiration did not contradict either their historical research or the free use of their minds. If we are to be true to what the Bible says about itself, we must recognize both the human and the divine authorship. Yet we must not allow either the divine or the human factor to take away from the other.

Divine inspiration did not override the human authorship. Human authorship did not override the divine inspiration. The Bible is equally God's words and human words. It is "God's word written",[4] God's word through human words, spoken by human mouths and written by human hands.

Recognition of the human element in Scripture means that we must read Scripture as literature. In saying this I am not saying that the Bible is no more than literature, which is the position of those who deny that it is either historically accurate or true and suggest that it consists merely of stories in which we can discover our story. They use the literary approach as an alternative to submitting to God's word.

The point I am making is that the human authors of Scripture used a range of human methods to communicate God's word. God could have moved them to write only lists of doctrines or commands, and the Bible certainly does contain these. But most of the time, God moved them to write history, stories, parables, poems and oracles. As preachers we need to remember that these literary forms are not incidental, accidental or irrelevant. They are part of what God intended. He arranged to have his truth conveyed through characters, settings, actions and images. Scripture aims to get the reader to share an experience, not just to grasp ideas. This may seem obvious, but many preachers need to be reminded of it for they treat the Bible as a mere storehouse of ideas. Such preachers impoverish it because they fail to see that the Bible is "human experience portrayed concretely".[5]

Once we are convinced that the literary form of the Bible is important, we who preach it should look at it even more closely. We are not just miners extracting ore and leaving the landscape desolate. We are skilled mapmakers, carefully observing the landscape of the text so that we can help our listeners see all its features and follow the paths and highways God has placed there. We often speak about ideas to our listeners – just as the Bible regularly does. But we should try to convey to our listeners as much of the tone and feeling, of the impressions and aims of the text as possible.

> The expository preacher ... approaches a biblical text on the premise that whatever was important enough for the writer to include in a text is important to the expositor as well. If

> rhetoric, style and special resources of language leap out at us from virtually every page of the Bible, we need to take note of them and do something with them when expounding the Bible. [6]

A corollary of this belief is that we have to be alert to the genre of a text and familiar with the rules of that genre. If I were to say, "Once upon a time ...", Western readers would recognize that I was going to tell a fairy story. Biblical writers also give us clues about what they are doing, and we need to make the effort to learn to recognize these clues. For instance, if the text tells a story, we must pay close attention to setting, characters, dialogue and plot. We must ask what this story contributes to the message of the biblical book in which it is found and to the Bible as a whole. If a passage is poetry, we must notice such things as imagery, compactness and parallel structures. If the text comes from a letter, we must think carefully about the situation that called for that letter and what its writer was aiming to do in this pastoral visit by post.

This literary approach calls for humility; we study each text as it is instead of as we might wish it to be. This includes trying to discover what the original speakers, writers and listeners would have understood. But the fruit of this hard work is that we understand the text better and preach it more faithfully. We also help our listeners to learn to handle the Bible properly.

The second belief to which we must hold is that *God still speaks through what he has spoken*. God is neither dead nor silent. Scripture is not just a collection of ancient documents in which the words of God are preserved, nor is it a kind of museum in which God's words are exhibited like relics or fossils. On the contrary, it is a living word to living people from the living God, a contemporary message for each generation.

The apostles clearly understood and believed this. They introduce their quotations from the Old Testament with one of two formulas. The one is "it is written". In Galatians 4:22 Paul says, "For it is written that Abraham had two sons". He is referring to something that was written down in the past and remains a permanent written record. The second is "it (or he) says", using a Greek tense that implies that God is still saying these words. For instance, in Galatians 4:21 Paul refers to "what the law says" and in Galatians 4:30 he asks, "What does Scripture say?" The "law" and "Scripture" are ancient books – how can they still be speaking? This is only possible because God himself speaks to us through it.

This truth is further emphasized in Hebrews 3:7 where the author quotes Psalm 95:7–11, beginning, "Today, if you hear his voice, do not harden your hearts". He introduces the quotation with the words "as the Holy Spirit says", implying that the Holy Spirit is asking people to listen to him today just as he did centuries ago when the psalm was written. Notice the four different occasions on which God is said to speak here: first in the wilderness when God spoke but Israel hardened her heart; then when the psalmist urged the people of his day not to repeat Israel's mistake; thirdly, when the Hebrew Christians of the first century A.D. were being encouraged, and, fourthly, as we read the Letter to the Hebrews today we hear God's plea. God's word moves with the times!

This principle also applies to the New Testament Scriptures. Each of the seven letters to the churches in Revelation 2 and 3 concludes with an identical plea: "Whoever has ears, let them hear what the Spirit says to the churches." Presumably each church heard its particular letter read aloud, and each knew that John had written that letter some time earlier on the island of Patmos. Yet each letter ended with the statement that the Spirit was still speaking to the churches. What was addressed to each church in particular also applied to all the churches in general. John's words had originated with the Holy Spirit and that Spirit was still speaking with a living voice to every church member who had ears to listen.

Grasping the truth that God still speaks through what he has spoken protects us from two opposite errors. The first is the belief that God's voice is silent today. The second is the belief that what God is saying today has little or nothing to do with Scripture. The truth is that God speaks through what he spoke. He himself makes his ancient word living and relevant to today.

Our final conviction about Scripture must be that *God's word is powerful*. When God speaks, he acts. His word does more than explain his action; it is active in itself. God achieves his purposes by his word (Isa 55:11). Given the glut of words that surround us every day, this may be difficult to believe. However, writers know that words are important and powerful. Alexander Solzhenitsyn – the Russian author who stood up to the power of the Kremlin and communism – knew this. In his speech as he accepted his Nobel Prize in 1970, he stated that "one word of truth outweighs the whole world".[7]

The other thing that may make us doubt the power of words is the accusation that the church talks too much and does too little. While we should examine ourselves to see if this is true, we should not abandon words. We need to remember that in the word of God speech and action are combined. God created the universe by his word: "he spoke, and it came to be; he commanded, and it stood firm" (Ps 33:9). Jesus, the Word of God, both preached and worked (Matt 4:23). And now through the same authoritative word, he recreates and saves. God uses his proclaimed message to save those who believe (1 Cor 1:21, 1 Thess 2:13).

The Bible presents many pictures of the power of God's word. It describes it as sharper than any two-edged sword, penetrating our mind and our conscience (Heb 4:12). Like a hammer, it can break stony hearts; like fire it can burn up rubbish (Jer 23:29). It lights our path, shining like a lamp on a dark night (Ps 119:105). Like a mirror it shows us both what we are and what we should be (Jas 1:22–25). It is compared to a seed leading to birth (Jas 1:18), to milk causing growth (1 Pet 2:2), to grain that nourishes whereas straw does not (Jer 23:28), to honey which sweetens and to gold which enriches its possessor (Ps 19:10).

These metaphors are not exaggerations. John Wesley's journal is full of references to the power of the word of God affecting people who were initially hostile to his preaching. Billy Graham saw the same power at work in his rallies. While we may not have the remarkable gifts of these great men, God's word is still powerful. We need to remember the parable of the sower. Not all our seed-sowing will bear fruit. Some ground is hard and stony, and the birds, the weeds and the scorching sun prevent the seed from growing. But we should be encouraged by the promise that some soil will prove good and will produce an abundance of lasting fruit. There is life and power in the seed, and when the Spirit prepares the soil and waters the seed, there will be growth and fruitfulness.

It can thus be said that "a true sermon is a real deed".[8] We enter the pulpit with a word in our hands, heart and mouth, and this word has power. We should expect results. We should look for conversions. Spurgeon urged pastors to "so pray and so preach that, if there are no conversions, you will be astonished, amazed and broken-hearted."[9]

Convictions about the Church

We have many convictions about the church, but here we focus on the firm belief that the church is the creation of God by his word and is dependent on his word. It is the word of God that keeps the church alive, directs and sanctifies it, reforms it and renews it. Christ rules and feeds his church through the word of God. Both as individuals and as a church, we "do not live on bread alone, but on every word that comes from the mouth of the Lord" (Deut 8:3, quoted by Jesus in Matt 4:4).

This point is made over and over again throughout the Scriptures as God addresses his people, teaching them his way, and appealing to them, for his sake and theirs, to hear and obey his message. The Old Testament constantly indicates that the welfare of God's people depends on their listening to his voice, believing his promises and obeying his commands. The health of the church in the New Testament also depended on their attentiveness to God's word.

This is still true today, despite the fact that we do not receive fresh, direct revelation as the prophets and apostles did. If we preach the Scriptures faithfully, the Holy Spirit will make the word of God live in the hearts of our hearers. Through his word God will give his people the vision without which the church will perish. First, they will begin to see that he wants his church to be his new society in the world. Then they will begin to grasp the resources he has given us in Christ to fulfil this purpose. Only by humble and obedient listening to his voice can the church grow to maturity, serve the world and glorify our Lord.

Martyn Lloyd-Jones pointed out that "the decadent periods and eras in the history of the church have always been those periods when preaching had declined".[10] A low level of Christian living is due, more than anything else, to a low level of Christian preaching. If the church is to flourish again, there is a need for faithful, powerful, biblical preaching. God still urges his people to listen and his preachers to proclaim his word.

Convictions about the Pastorate

Jesus Christ gives leaders to his church and intends them to be a permanent part of the church's structure. We need to heed Paul's words: "Here is a trustworthy statement: whoever aspires to be an overseer desires a noble task" (1 Tim 3:1).

The New Testament refers to the leaders of the church as overseers or elders (Titus 1:5). They are no longer Old Testament priests offering sacrifices, but are pastors or shepherds whose chief responsibility is to care for their flock (Acts 20:28). God rebuked the shepherds of Israel for feeding themselves instead of their sheep (Ezek 34:1–3), but the Good Shepherd not only promised that his sheep would be safe in his care, but also repeatedly instructed Peter to "feed my lambs" and "feed my sheep" (John 10:9; 21:15–17). This was a command the apostles never forgot. Peter later wrote that the elders must "be shepherds of God's flock" (1 Pet 5:2), and Paul told the elders of the Ephesian church: "Keep watch over yourselves and all the flock of which the Holy Spirit has made you overseers. Be shepherds of the church of God" (Acts 20:28). What a privilege to be asked by the Chief Shepherd to care for those whom he had bought with his own blood!

To feed God's flock means to teach his church, which is why the requirements for being an elder include both loyalty to the apostolic faith and a gift for teaching (Titus 1:9; 1 Tim 3:2). This teaching must not be done in such a domineering way that the congregation becomes more dependent on the elder than on the Spirit of truth (Matt 23:8). After all, God's new covenant promises that "they will all know me" as the Holy Spirit is given to all believers. All "have an anointing from the Holy One" and "have been taught by God" and therefore in a sense we do not need human teachers (Jer 31:34; 1 John 2:20–27; 1 Thess 4:9). It is also true that all church members have a responsibility to "let the message of Christ dwell among you richly as you teach and admonish one another with all wisdom" (Col 3:16). Yet all these truths do not contradict the fact that pastors are called and set apart to devote themselves to a work of preaching and teaching (1 Tim 5:17).

The fact that the Lord's gifts to his church include "pastors and teachers" (Eph 4:11) indicates that God wants every local church to have the benefit of pastoral oversight. This oversight should be exercised by a team, for the word "elders" is nearly always in the plural in the New Testament (Acts 14:23, 20:17; 1 Tim 4:14; Titus 1:5). The elders' task includes preaching and teaching, and at least one team member should embrace the demanding work of preaching the word. This task demands much time and energy, but without such commitment the congregation is likely to be weak and unfed.

The question sometimes arises of whether there is a difference between teaching and preaching. If there is, it is very minor. Jesus both taught and preached (Matt 4:23) and the Apostle Paul described himself as both a preacher and a teacher of the gospel (Titus 1:3; 2 Tim 1:11). His preaching may have been aimed at sinners and his teaching at his converts. But the content of his preaching does not seem entirely different from the content of his teaching. There was probably a good deal of overlap.

It is also sometimes said when the New Testament refers to preaching, it is referring to evangelism and that what we call preaching (a sermon to a Christian congregation) does not occur in the New Testament. But a brief historical survey will show the weakness of this argument.

The practice of bringing the people of God together to have his word explained to them goes back to the Old Testament. Moses instructed the priests to gather the people and read the law to them, presumably explaining and applying it as they went along (Deut 31:9–13; see also Mal 2:7–9). Ezra "brought the Law before the assembly" and "read it aloud". The Levites shared his ministry and "read from the book of the Law of God, making it clear and giving the meaning so that the people understood" (Neh 8:1–8). Later, the synagogue services included readings from the Law and the Prophets, after which somebody preached. When Jesus was in the synagogue at Nazareth, he first read from Isaiah 61 and then in his message announced that he was the fulfilment of this Scripture (Luke 4:16–22). Likewise when Paul attended the synagogue in Pisidian Antioch, the worshippers first listened to a reading "from the Law and the Prophets", after which Paul was invited to preach (Acts 13:14–43).

When believers either left or were thrown out of the synagogues and began to arrange their own Christian meetings, they kept the same form of service. However, they added to the extracts from the Law and the Prophets a reading from one of the apostles' letters (e.g. Col 4:16; 1

Thess 5:27). Luke gives us a glimpse of a Christian assembly at Troas where the worship included the breaking of bread and a sermon from Paul who "kept on talking until midnight", with disastrous consequences (Acts 20:7–11).

Although this is the only Christian worship service in the New Testament that is specifically said to have included a sermon, there is no reason to suppose that it was exceptional. On the contrary, Paul gives Timothy specific instructions about preaching: "Until I come, devote yourself to the public reading of Scripture, to preaching and to teaching" (1 Tim 4:13). It is clear that the reading from the Bible was to be followed by both preaching and instruction based on the Scripture passage. Probably there was some evangelism as well, for those present would have included fringe members (known as "God-fearers" in the synagogues), those who were preparing for baptism, and even unbelieving visitors (1 Cor 14:23). Yet the emphasis was on teaching the faithful.

If today's pastors were to take the New Testament emphasis on preaching and teaching seriously, they would find their work extremely fulfilling. Instead, sadly, many pastors are more involved in administration. The symbols of their ministry are the office rather than the study, and the telephone, computer and Blackberry rather than the Bible. Making "prayer and the ministry of the word" our priority, as the apostles did (Acts 6:4), might involve a radical restructuring of our daily and weekly tasks. We would have to delegate more responsibilities to lay leaders. But it would show a truly New Testament attitude and approach to the pastorate and would greatly improve the health of the church.

Convictions about Preaching

What sorts of sermon should pastors preach? Textbooks tend to list options, one of which may be an expository sermon. But I cannot agree that this is just one possible type among many. All true Christian preaching should be expository. We misuse this word if we think it applies only to a verse-by-verse explanation of a lengthy passage of Scripture. In reality, "expository" refers to the content of the sermon rather than its style. To "expound" Scripture means to bring out what is in the text, to reveal it. The expositor opens what seems to be closed, makes plain what is confusing, unravels what is knotted, and unfolds what is tightly packed.

This "text" might be a word, a verse, or a sentence. Sometimes it will be a paragraph or two. It might even be a whole chapter or book. The size of the text does not matter, so long as it is from the Bible. What matters is what we do with it. Whether it is long or short, our responsibility as expositors is to open it up in such a way that it speaks its own message clearly, plainly, accurately, relevantly, without addition, subtraction or twisting. In expository preaching the biblical text is not a launching pad for a sermon that goes on to handle a very different theme. Neither is it a convenient peg on which to hang a jumble of thoughts. The text is a master which dictates and controls the content, tone and aim of our sermons. Philip Ryken says it well:

> Expository preaching is not so much a method as it is a mindset. A minister who sees himself as an expositor knows that he is not the master of the word but its servant. He has no other ambition than to preach what the Scriptures actually teach. His aim is to be faithful to God's word so that his people can hear God's voice. He himself is only God's mouthpiece, speaking God's message into the ears of God's people, and thus into their minds and hearts. To that end, he carefully works his way through the Scriptures, reading, explaining, and applying them to his congregation.[11]

David Hubbard captures how this humble attitude works in practice:

> Interpreting the Bible is like safecracking. Not the kind where you go in with crowbars and dynamite, but the kind when, with filed fingers, you feel the knob until the tumblers drop. You let the safe give you its own combination. As we deal with the Scripture in our preparation we have to be honest with it. Our tendency is to have an idea … And then we say, "Now if I can find a text or a passage to support that idea." A great deal of our preaching falls into the trap of putting the Bible to a utilitarian purpose. We use the text as an instrument to back up some ideas that we want to put across rather than going to the text and letting that text inform us.[12]

Let us consider some of the main benefits of this disciplined approach.

First, *exposition sets us limits*. It restricts us to the scriptural text. We are not expounding a passage from the world's literature, or from a political speech, or even from a religious book. Nor are we presenting our own opinions. No, our text is always taken from God's word. The very first qualification for expository preaching is the recognition that we are guardians of a sacred "deposit" of truth (1 Tim 6:20; 2 Tim 1:12–14), trustees of the gospel (1 Thess 2:4), "stewards of the mysteries of God"; (1 Cor 4:1, 2 KJV).

Secondly, *exposition demands integrity*. Sadly not everybody is convinced of this. It is said that the Bible can be made to mean anything one wants, but this is only true if one lacks integrity and does not engage in disciplined study.

The description of what we do as grammatico-historical exegesis reminds us that we have to interpret the text in the light of its historical origin and its grammar. When the sixteenth-century Reformers began to refer to the "literal" interpretation of the Scriptures, they were not denying that some passages are poetic and figurative, but were contrasting their approach with the fanciful allegorical style of interpretation. They were emphasizing that every Bible student must look for the plain, natural, obvious meaning of each text. What did the original author intend his words to mean? That was the question – a question which can be answered confidently, if we work patiently. The biblical authors were honest men, not deceivers, and they intended their writings to be understood.

The Reformers also argued that Scripture has a unity given it by God and that it must, therefore, be allowed to interpret itself. One passage will shed light on another. Christians must respect this harmony and should not interpret any passage in a way that contradicts another. We recognize that there are difficult passages, but we should seek to harmonize them in a responsible way.

It would be a good thing if every Christian preacher could say with John Calvin, "I have not corrupted one single passage of Scripture, nor twisted it as far as I know ... and I have always studied to be simple".[13]

John Bright also tackles the problem of integrity when he says that a biblical preacher must begin by taking the trouble to determine exactly what his text means:

not what he had always thought it meant, not what he would prefer it to mean, not what it may seem on the surface to mean, but what it actually means. There can be no biblical preaching if the text is not taken with utmost seriousness. If the preacher feels free to disregard his text, if he allows himself to twist or slant its meaning in order to have it support some point he wishes to make, or if he is content to derive incidental lessons from it while ignoring what it principally intended to say, he should give up all pretense of doing biblical preaching. Biblical preaching is a preaching that aims to bring the text's own word to bear on the contemporary situation; it must therefore begin with the text's own words. It demands that the preacher make a manful effort to ascertain as precisely as he can what the text intended to convey to those to whom it was originally addressed. If he will not trouble to do that, he can derive no legitimate message from the text for his congregation. His sermon may be interesting, perhaps even edifying; but let him not advertise it as the authentic biblical word to his people. It represents no more than his own words, his own reflections, perhaps as these were suggested by the biblical word, and he ought frankly to admit it.[14]

Thirdly, *exposition identifies the traps* we must avoid. The two main pitfalls are forgetfulness and disloyalty. The forgetful expositor loses sight of his text when he follows his own ideas and forgets to follow what the text says. The disloyal expositor appears to stick to his text, but strains and stretches it so that it means something quite different from its original and natural meaning. The New Testament writers themselves use word pictures to warn us against this wickedness. False teachers are condemned for "swerving" from the truth, like an archer who misses the target (2 Tim 2:18, ESV); They "peddle" God's word, like a tradesman who sells by trickery (2 Cor 2:17). They "pervert" the gospel by altering its content, and "distort" or twist the Scriptures into an unrecognizable shape (Gal 1:7; 2 Pet 3:16). By contrast Paul declares that he has "renounced secret and shameful ways", that he utterly refuses to "distort the word of God", and that instead he sets "forth the truth plainly" (2 Cor 4:2).

Fourthly, *exposition gives us confidence to preach.* If we were offering our own views or those of some imperfect fellow human being, we would do so hesitantly. But if we are honestly expounding God's word, we can be very bold. Whoever speaks, wrote Peter, should do so "as one who speaks the very words of God" (1 Pet 4:11). We, like the Jews, have been "entrusted with the very words of God" (Rom 3:2). Our main task is to handle these words so faithfully that God can still speak through them.

The truths that have been presented in this chapter about God, the Scriptures, the church, the pastorate and biblical exposition should strengthen our trembling beliefs. Today's objections and challenges to preaching should not put us off. Instead, we should give ourselves to this ministry with fresh energy and determination. Nothing should distract us from our great task.

3

PREACHING AS
BRIDGE-BUILDING

So far we have discussed some current challenges to preaching and developed a theological defence of it. But we have not yet defined what preaching is, except to insist that if it is to be really Christian it must be expository. Yet this is not a complete definition. Preaching is far more than just interpreting biblical texts.

This becomes clear when we look at six of the main metaphors used to describe Christian preachers. The commonest is that of the herald or town crier, who has been given some good news and told to announce it to everyone. So he goes to the marketplace or public square and makes the news known. Paul describes his own preaching as heralding Christ crucified (1 Cor 1:23) and heralding Jesus Christ as Lord (2 Cor 4:5; see also Isa 40:9; 52:7).

Preachers are also described as sowers who go out into the world like farmers going into their fields. They sow the precious seed of God's word, hoping and praying that some of it will fall into well-prepared soil and in due course bear good fruit (Luke 8:4–15).

They are ambassadors appointed to plead the cause of a ruler or government in a foreign, or even hostile, land (2 Cor 5:20; Eph 6:20). They are also stewards or housekeepers who have been put in charge of God's household and entrusted with provisions to be faithfully shared with the members of the household (1 Cor 4:1, 2; 1 Tim 3:4, 5; Titus 1:7).

We have already talked about their role as pastors or shepherds. The Chief Shepherd has entrusted the care of his flock to them, and as under-shepherds they must protect the flock from wolves (false teachers) and lead them to pasture (sound teaching) (Ezek 34; John 21:15–17; Acts 20:28–31).

The sixth metaphor presents the preacher as "a worker who does not need to be ashamed" because he "handles the word of truth" skilfully (2 Tim 2:15). In other contexts, the Greek verb used here means "able to cut a straight path through country that is forested or difficult to pass through so that a traveller can go directly to his destination".[15] This straight teaching contrasts with the false teaching of those who swerve from the truth (2 Tim 2:18, ESV). Our exposition must be faithful and simple so that our hearers can understand and follow it easily.

Notice that in each of these six pictures the message is given. Preachers are not to invent it; it has been entrusted to them. The good news has been given to the herald to announce, the good seed to the farmer to sow, the good food to the steward to hand out, and good grazing is available for the shepherd's flock. Similarly, ambassadors do not present their own ideas but the policies of their country. Workers cut a way for "the word of truth", not for their own words. In all these New Testament images, the preacher is a servant under someone else's authority, the communicator of someone else's word. The preacher's task is to contextualize this message, relaying it in such a way that listeners can relate to it.

Crossing the Cultural Gulf

The biblical metaphors show that preaching is the communicating of a God-given message to our contemporaries, who need to hear it. To be able to do this, we need to be able to build bridges spanning the chasm between the biblical world and the modern world. Just as a bridge makes it possible for traffic to flow from one side of a river or ravine to another, so our preaching must make it possible for God's revealed truth to flow out of the Scriptures and into the lives of men and women today. Both ends of our bridges must be firmly rooted if we are to be able to show that Christianity is still relevant today.

Preachers who are theologically conservative tend to make the mistake of living only on the Bible side of the gulf. That is where we feel comfortable and safe. We believe the Bible, love the Bible, read the Bible, study the Bible and preach the Bible message. But we are not at home in the modern world on the other side of the gulf. It bewilders and threatens us. So our bridge is firmly rooted in the Bible but never reaches the other side. If we are called to account for our practice of exposition without application, we piously reply that our trust is in the Holy Spirit to apply his word to the realities of human life.

On the other side of the chasm are the preachers who are proud to be moving with the times and who ground their sermons in the modern world. They are very anxious to restate the Christian faith in terms which are understandable, meaningful and believable to their contemporaries, and so they try to answer the questions people are asking even when they are the wrong questions. But if we uncritically accept the world's own self-understanding, we may find ourselves the servants of the latest trend instead of the servants of God. In our eagerness to be relevant, we may disregard God's revealed truth.

So we find that conservatives are biblical but not contemporary, while liberals and radicals are modern but not biblical. And nobody seems to be building bridges. We must ask God to make us Christian communicators who are determined to bridge the ravine. We must struggle to relate God's unchanging word to our ever-changing world without sacrificing truth or despising relevance.

In building such bridges, we are simply following the example of God, who communicated to his people in their specific historical and cultural situations through his prophets, and whose eternal Word became flesh as a first-century Palestinian Jew. God reached down to people. He demonstrated that we who preach must not just use the language of our listeners, but actually enter their worlds of thought and feeling. Incarnation (exchanging one world for another), not just translation (exchanging one language for another) is the Christian model of communication.

In building bridges, we are also following in the footsteps of the great preachers in every age. Chrysostom (who died in 407) is described as a "man of the word and a man of the world" whose preaching was both timeless and timely.[16] Jonathan Edward in the eighteenth century is said to have had an unrivalled knowledge of the Bible and of the human heart.[17] Both Spurgeon in the nineteenth century and Karl Barth in the twentieth advised preachers to prepare with "the Bible in one hand and the daily newspaper in the other".[18]

But bridge-building is not the only metaphor that can be used for connecting the Bible and the world. Ian Pitt-Watson offers another image:

> Every sermon is stretched like a bowstring between the text of the Bible on the one hand and the problems of contemporary human life on the other. If the string is insecurely tethered to either end, the bow is useless.[19]

Yet another image is offered by Bishop Stephen Neill:

> Preaching is like weaving. There are the two factors of the warp and the woof. There is the fixed, unalterable element, which for us is the word of God, and there is the variable element, which enables the weaver to change and vary the pattern at his will. For us that variable element is the constantly changing pattern of people and of situations.[20]

Preaching Christ

If our preaching is to build a bridge between the Bible and the world, the first thing we must do is tackle the major themes of human life: What is the purpose of our existence? Has life any significance? Where did I come from? Where am I going to? What does it mean to be human? How do people differ from animals? Why do all people long to worship? What is freedom? Why is there a painful gap between what I am and what I long to be? Is there a way to get rid of guilt and shame? Why do we hunger for love, sexual fulfilment, marriage, family life and community, but also experience destructive passions like jealousy, malice, hate, lust and revenge? Why do we feel alienated from others? Is it possible to love my neighbour? Why do evil and suffering exist? How can we find courage to face life, death, and what may lie beyond death? What hope can encourage us in our despair?

These questions have been asked in every generation. They reflect the nature of humanity as revealed in Scripture: we are dignified creatures made in God's image, but also fallen and guilty sinners.

Jesus Christ either provides the answers to these questions or throws more light on deep mysteries such as pain and evil than anyone else does. He is the fulfilment of every human desire (Col 2:3, 9–10). Therefore, above all else, we must preach Christ. If we want to find true wisdom, to enter into a right relationship with God, or to grow in character, we must turn to Jesus Christ. For Christ crucified and risen has been appointed by God to satisfy his people.

The one we preach is not Christ-in-a-vacuum, not a remote being unrelated to the real world, not just the Jesus of history. He is the risen Christ who once lived and died, and now lives and rules. He gives us a sense of self-worth because he assures us of God's love for us. He sets us free from guilt and shame because he died for us. We escape from the prison of our self-centredness by the power of his resurrection. We need not live in fear, because he reigns. He gives meaning to marriage and home, to work and leisure, to individuality and citizenship. He promises us that history is neither meaningless nor endless. One day he will return to end it, to destroy death and to bring a new universe of righteousness and peace.

Preaching Ethics

Bridge-building also requires us to address the ethical and social issues that affect our hearers and the society in which we live, for the gospel is not just about our salvation but also about our sanctification. James insists that "faith without deeds is dead" (Jas 2:26).

Ethical behaviour is not an automatic consequence of accepting the good news. It has to be taught. That is why the apostles who proclaimed the gospel also gave clear and concrete ethical instruction. To teach the standards of moral conduct that adorn the gospel and insist that our hearers heed them is neither legalism nor pharisaism but plain apostolic Christianity.

This responsibility of preachers is clearly laid out in Paul's letter to Titus, where Titus is instructed both to teach "what is appropriate to sound doctrine" (the apostolic faith) and also to encourage good behaviour to "make the teaching about God our Saviour more attractive" (moral behaviour). In Titus 2:1–10, Paul gives detailed instructions for different groups in the congregation. The older men are to behave responsibly and be kind, serious and mature. The older women are to be reverent and teach the younger wives about their responsibilities to their husbands and children. Titus himself is to set the young men a good example and to urge them to be self-controlled. Slaves are to please their masters by being hardworking and honest. These instructions make it clear that when we proclaim the gospel, we must go on to unfold its moral consequences. Similarly, when we teach Christian behaviour, we must lay its gospel foundations.

In our preaching, we need to deal with how our faith affects our moral behaviour in a number of spheres, starting with the *individual* sphere. We need to consider our duty to our bodies as the Holy Spirit's temple when deciding whether to smoke or get a tattoo or a piercing. Given that the discipline of the eyes is a major means to sexual self-control, we have to make a conscientious choice about what films to see, what magazines to read and what Web sites to surf. In relation to dress, we have to distinguish between modesty and vanity, simplicity and extravagance. But when preaching on these issues, we must be careful not to lose our sense of proportion. In comparison with the big moral and social issues of the day, some of these matters are secondary at best. To become preoccupied with them is to be guilty of a pharisaism that majors on minors and neglects what Jesus called "the more important matters of the law – justice, mercy and faithfulness" (Matt 23:23, 24). Yet we must still point out that the Old Testament sets out what it means to live according to the Ten Commandments. We must be like John the Baptist in the New Testament, who told people what it meant to "produce fruits in keeping with repentance". Tax-gatherers were to collect only the money actually owed. Soldiers were neither to extort money nor accuse people falsely, and were to be content with their pay (Luke 3:8–14). The apostles gave similar teaching in their letters, which sometimes commend the general Christian virtues ("love, joy, peace, patience, kindness, goodness, faithfulness, gentleness and self-control" – Gal 5:22, 23) and sometimes give specific instructions about such things as controlling our tongues (Jas 3:1–12).

We also have responsibilities to each other within the *church*, the new community. Much of the apostles' moral teaching dealt with "how people ought to conduct themselves in God's household" (1 Tim 3:15).

Here is where all the "one another" commands in the New Testament apply. We are to love one another, forgive and tolerate one another, encourage and correct one another, "offer hospitality to one another without grumbling" (1 Pet 4:9) and "carry each other's burdens" (Gal 6:2). Paul also provides a whole list of duties in Ephesians 4 and 5, telling us to do away with falsehood, anger, dishonesty, evil talk, bitterness, gossip and impurity. As "members of one body" (4:25), all our behaviour must reflect our unity.

As members of *families*, we must show moral behaviour in our homes. Both Paul and Peter outline the duties of husbands and wives, parents and children, masters and slaves (Eph 5:21–6:9; Col 3:18–4:1; 1 Pet 2:18–3:7). They clearly feel strongly about the Christian home and the relationships there and give straightforward instruction about this. So should we, for marriage, parenthood and work are still a major part of life and are daily concerns of nearly everyone in Christian congregations. Because Christian standards differ greatly from those in the non-Christian world, Christians will be witnessing to their communities as they live out these beliefs and standards.

As members of *communities and of the human race*, we also need to address the major issues in our world today. For example, we cannot simplistically confine the teaching of the Sermon on the Mount to the realm of individual ethics. It raises questions about issues such as violence and non-violence in the community that cannot either be dodged in our own thinking or be eliminated from the pulpit. We have to consider how our Lord's teaching about loving our enemies instead of taking revenge (Matt 5:38–48) applies to our personal responses in the violent world in which we live. What does it mean in terms of our countries and politicians, governors, law-makers, policemen, judges, and so forth? We should note that Paul deliberately contrasts the duty of individual Christians not to "repay anyone evil for evil" and the duty of the state to punish evildoers (Rom 12:17–13:5). He instructs us not to take revenge, not because revenge is wrong but because it is God's right to take revenge, not ours.

There are several other issues that cannot be avoided in our preaching. One such issue is sexual behaviour. Certain standards of sexual morality are clearly taught in the Bible. We learn, for instance, that sexual intercourse belongs only in lifelong heterosexual marriage

(Gen 2:24; Mark 10:5–9; 1 Thess 4:3–5). What is more, since marriage was established at creation, these divine standards apply to everybody, not just to believers. It is impossible, therefore, to limit the faithful teaching of biblical sex ethics to the congregation; we also have to be involved in public discussion about marriage, about divorce, about the remarriage of divorced persons, and about homosexual partnerships.

Christians should discuss these issues thoroughly and should use the pulpit to do so clearly and bravely. Preachers have a duty to expound God's standards and encourage their congregations to uphold them. Furthermore, we must present these standards to the non-Christian community. We must preach and defend the gospel, but we must also teach and defend biblical sexual ethics. They are essential to a society's health; failure to keep to them destroys a nation and a community.[21]

Jesus also spoke much of the dangers of loving and serving wealth, the sin of envy, the foolishness of materialism and the duty of generosity. James includes in his letter a fierce condemnation of rich people who cling to their wealth, fail to pay their workers and live in selfish luxury (Jas 5:1–6). Like John and Paul, he emphasizes that Christians with many possessions are to share with the poor to ensure that they have the necessities of life (Jas 2:14–18; 1 John 3:17, 18; 2 Cor 8:1–15). There are hundreds of deprived people in our world today. The huge economic gap between the developed and the developing nations and between rich and poor must concern Christians. God is concerned about the unity of the human race, the wasting of the earth's riches and the injustice of inequality.

When we begin to discuss these issues, we enter the field of politics. It is not enough simply to try to alleviate suffering. We also need to address issues of injustice, poverty, hunger, illiteracy and disease; the pollution of the environment; failure to conserve natural resources; abortion, mercy-killing or euthanasia and capital punishment; inhumane technocracy, bureaucracy and unemployment; nationalism and tribalism; violence and revolution; the arms race, nuclear proliferation and the threat of biological warfare and terrorism; the increase of crime and our responsibility for the criminal; racism. The list seems almost endless. How can we ban such topics from the pulpit? If we do so in order to concentrate on spiritual topics, we are suggesting that God is concerned only about spiritual matters but not about the welfare of his creation.

To do so is to divorce Christian faith from Christian life. We would be guilty of encouraging Christians to withdraw from the real world and would justify Marx's well-known criticism that religion is an opiate which drugs people into acquiescing in the status quo.

I am not saying that we are to promote precise political programmes from the pulpit. Rather, it is the preacher's responsibility to lay out biblical principles so that everyone can develop Christian values. Opinion-formers and policy-makers in the congregation need to be inspired and encouraged to apply these principles wherever they have influence. Our task is to help Christians develop a Christian mind, to lead them into maturity. We need to encourage our listeners to be the salt of the world, preventing social decay. We should urge them to spread the light of Christ's love, peace and righteousness and so to help shape a society which is more pleasing to the God of compassion and justice.

The pulpit always has political influence, even if nothing remotely connected with politics is ever said there. A preacher's silence suggests that he supports what is going on in society. Instead of helping to change society and make it more pleasing to God, the pulpit is then simply a mirror that reflects society, and the church conforms to the world. The pulpit cannot be neutral. Our task is not to avoid issues, nor to provide quick and easy answers. We need wisdom not to go beyond what is written in Scripture and to speak carefully where Scripture is not clear. But humility and wisdom must never keep us from discussing the urgent issues facing our world today.

4

THE CALL TO STUDY

If we are to build bridges and relate the word of God to the major themes of life and the major issues of today, we have to take both the Bible and today's world seriously. To withdraw from the world into the Bible (escapism) or from the Bible into the world (conformity) will be fatal to our preaching. Our responsibility is to explore the landscape on both sides of the ravine until we are familiar with the territory. Only then shall we see the connections between them. Only then will we be able to speak God's word into the human situation with authority, wisdom, sensitivity and accuracy.

This exploration means studying. The best teachers remain students all their lives. Spurgeon said it well: "He who has ceased to learn has ceased to teach. He who no longer sows in the study will no more reap in the pulpit."[22] Billy Graham quoted a preacher who said: "If I had only three years to serve the Lord, I would spend two of them studying and preparing." Without study, our breath is stale and our touch clumsy; with study, our sermons will "be like the leaping of a fountain, and not like the pumping of a pump".[23] Freshness and sparkle come from study.

Bible Study

Since as pastors we are chiefly called to preach the word, the study of Scripture is one of our greatest responsibilities. Only when we have absorbed it can we confidently proclaim it. God spoke to Samuel when he listened; then, when Samuel spoke to Israel, they listened to him (1

Sam 3:19–4:1). Before Ezekiel was able to speak God's word to others, he himself had to swallow and digest it (Ezek 3:1).

The more we value the Bible, the more careful and conscientious our study of it should be, for it takes time and focus to ensure that the text opens up its treasures. Our study must be *comprehensive*. Merely dipping into the Scriptures is not enough. Nor must we limit ourselves to our favourite passages or concentrate on the microscopic examination of a few key passages. Such use of Scripture plays into the devil's hands. Every heresy or false teaching arises from overemphasising some truth, without allowing other truths to balance it. Instead, we must study a wide variety of passages before drawing general conclusions. In this way we can make sure that our theology is sound and biblical and that the grand themes of Scripture become clear. Then, in turn, we will see these themes in the individual passages. So, knowledge of the parts helps us to see the big picture, and the big picture helps us see what is in each part.

How can we get to know the whole Bible thoroughly? A good place to start is by using the McCheyne Bible reading calendar, produced in 1842 and reproduced in Appendix 2 at the back of this book. This scheme enables one to read the whole Bible through every year, the Old Testament once and the New Testament twice. Four chapters are to be read daily, two in the morning and two in the evening. What is particularly helpful is the way in which McCheyne allocates the chapters. We start on 1 January with the four great beginnings of Scripture: Genesis 1 (the birth of creation), Ezra 1 (the rebirth of the nation), Matthew 1 (the birth of the Christ) and Acts 1 (the birth of the church). In this way we follow the parallel lines of God's unfolding purpose.[24] This reading plan provides an extremely valuable way to survey the landscape of Scripture and grasp its underlying and recurring themes.

Our study of the Bible must also be *humble*. We must genuinely desire to hear and obey God's word, without twisting its meaning or avoiding its challenge. How is this possible? How can I, who have been brought up in one culture, take a particular biblical text that was given in an ancient culture and interpret it without twisting the message? What are we to do about this cultural distance?

To begin with, we have to use our knowledge and imagination to transport ourselves back into the biblical writer's situation. We need to think what he thought and feel what he felt. Our responsibility is not to adjust his views to ours, by reading our opinions into what he wrote, but to adjust our views to his, by struggling to enter into his heart and mind. To do this, we need more than just imaginative insight into his situation; we also need insight into our own. We do not come to the biblical text as innocent, objective, impartial, culture-free investigators. We are nothing of the kind! No, the reading-glasses through which we look at the Bible have cultural lenses. And the mind with which we think about the Bible, however open we keep it, is not empty! Instead, it is filled with cultural prejudices. We must be aware of these, even though we cannot ever escape them. We should pray earnestly that we do not read into the Bible the views and philosophies of the world, such as humanism, Marxism and capitalism.

The questions we bring to the Bible and the answers we expect to get are both shaped by our cultural background. "What is received back, however, will not be answers only, but more questions. ... We find that our culturally conditioned presuppositions are being challenged and our questions corrected. In fact, we are compelled to re-formulate our previous questions and to ask fresh ones."[25] We have to open our minds wide enough to risk hearing what we do not want to hear. We have to be willing to let God decide what he wants to say to us, however uncomfortable we may find it. We have to break down the cultural barriers, and struggle to open our hearts and minds to listen to whatever he has to say.

Thirdly, our Bible study needs to be expectant. Sadly, expectancy can be blocked by pessimism. The interpretation of Scripture may appear so complicated that we despair of ever gaining a true and balanced understanding of God's word. But Scripture is intended for ordinary people like us. Consider 1 Corinthians with all its deep teaching on doctrine, morals and church order. It was written to a Christian community where "not many of you were wise by human standards" (1 Cor 1:26). Be patient! God will enable us to understand the Bible, if we study it faithfully.

Spiritual staleness also blocks our expectancy. This can be a major problem for all pastors. If we read through the whole Bible annually, after a few years we feel we know it fairly well. We may come to our daily reading with no very lively expectation that God is going to speak to us through it. Yet we should be confident that God has "more truth and light yet to break forth out of his holy word".[26] We need to ask God to waken our ears as he did for Isaiah (50:4). We need, like Samuel, to say "speak, for your servant is listening" (1 Sam 3:10). We need to "call out for insight and cry aloud for understanding", to "look for it as for silver and search for it as for hidden treasure". Then we shall understand and "find the knowledge of God" (Prov 2:3–5). We need to keep going. Like Jacob, we must hold onto God and refuse to let him go until he blesses us (Gen 32:26). God honours this spirit of eager and determined expectation. He promises to fill the hungry with good things; it is only the self-satisfied whom he sends away empty (Luke 1:53). So we must not give in to spiritual staleness as if it were normal or tolerable. We must pray that the Holy Spirit will light the fires of expectancy in us again.

Although the Bible itself is always our textbook, we should also take advantage of all the available aids to understanding. How widely we can read will depend on the availability of good books, the time we have, and where we feel an interest or a need.

We would be wise to read old books as well as new, especially the Christian classics that have been tested over the years. Some of these are often included in Bible software packages, or are available in full on the Internet. These books are often more valuable than recent popular books, although it is important to be able to guide our congregations about modern writings too. Some knowledge of historical theology will also give us a background from which to view the latest doctrinal fashions. Few truths or heresies are new; most are simply old ideas said in a new way. Reading biographies can also bring balance, wisdom and encouragement as we learn how God has dealt with Christians in other times and places. Our aim in all this reading should not so much be to gather knowledge as to develop our Christian mind.

Books are expensive. If there is a good public library nearby, use it. See if it offers interlibrary loans, which will make it possible for you to order almost any book you want. Read articles and journals on the Internet, taking care to check that they come from reliable sources. Electronic books are already a blessing to some, and may become more widely available. Ideally, the local church should develop a small lending and reference library. Pastors can also lend books to one another and to their church members. Concentrate on collecting essential reference books, especially dictionaries and commentaries to which you will turn again and again.[27] All the better if they are written for your own culture, like the one-volume *Africa Bible Commentary*,[28] the soon-to-be published *South Asia Bible Commentary*, the *Latin America Bible Commentary* and the *Arabic Contemporary Commentary*.

We should also make the most of pastors' gatherings, and preachers' clubs where we can encourage one another in study. The most famous of these was started in 1783 by John Newton, the ex-slave-trader who became a pastor. After tea and prayer, the group discussed "for about three hours on a proposed subject". Newton commented that the group should be called the Royal Society because they were all members of God's royal family and "the King himself condescends to meet with us".[29] All over the world such groups still meet to share what they have learned from Scripture and to help one another become better preachers.

The Contemporary World

Biblical and theological studies alone, however, do not make for good preaching. They provide an essential foundation, but unless we also study contemporary society we can be disastrously isolated on one side of the ravine. Our study of the today's world begins with people, not books. The best preachers are always diligent pastors, who know their congregations and the people of their area. These pastors understand life with its pain and pleasure, glory and tragedy. The quickest way to gain this understanding is to shut our mouths (a hard task for some of us preachers!) and open our eyes and ears. It has been said that God gives us two ears and two eyes but only one mouth, so he obviously intends us to look and listen twice as much as we talk!

We need to ask people questions and get them talking. We ought to know more about the Bible than they do, but they are likely to know more about the world than we do. So we should encourage them to tell us about their home and family life, their job, their expertise and their interests. We also need to hear about their thinking. How does their Christian faith motivate them? What problems prevent them from believing or from applying their faith to their life? The more varied their backgrounds, the more we have to learn. Listen to the different generations. Listen to different cultures. Such humble listening is essential. Our knowledge of the Bible and other people's knowledge of the world combine to construct bridges and ensure that our preaching is relevant.

In addition, we should read a newspaper or news magazine, follow in-depth web or radio news reports, watch some television and, where possible, discover what books are influencing our listeners most so that we can read them too. We may also find it helpful to see some of the better films and plays that mirror our society.

However, Jesus' teaching about the offending eye, foot or hand still applies (Matt 5:29–30). So it is sensible to make careful enquiries before reading books or seeing plays or films. In cases where the spirit of antichrist is dangerously subtle, it may be helpful to go with a group of friends who will make it easier to remain detached and so avoid being sucked into the atmosphere.

Even if we feel that we are strong enough to withstand pollution, we must consider the weak conscience of a brother or sister and must not make them stumble. If, therefore, we have those in our congregation who would be offended by our going to the theatre or cinema, it is up to us to educate or "strengthen" their consciences by patiently teaching sound doctrine. It must be clear that we are not co-operating with the spirit of the age but trying to understand it so that our preaching can be relevant.

Reading and Resource Groups

What else can we do to increase our understanding of today's world? I can testify to the immense value I have received over the years from a small reading group of about a dozen young graduates, professionals and post-graduate students. At each monthly meeting we would decide what we would read before the next meeting. We then spent an evening together, sharing our reactions to the book, discussing its message and implications, and trying to develop a Christian response to it. Some of the chosen books were written from a Christian perspective, but we concentrated on non-religious books because the main purpose of the group was to help us understand the non-Christian mind.

I recommend this approach. In almost every congregation there are surely a few thoughtful people who could meet with their pastor occasionally to discuss the relationship between the church and the world, the Christian mind and the non-Christian mind, Jesus Christ and his rivals. Resource groups of experts in areas of concern are also of tremendous value to a busy pastor.

Habits of Study

We have to study both the ancient text and the present scene, both Scripture and culture, both the word and the world. It is a huge task, demanding a lifetime of study. How can it be done? In times past, ministers managed it mostly by avoiding distracting duties. Joseph Parker, the first minister of the City Temple in London, began his studies at seven-thirty every morning and refused to get involved in public life or business. "I have lived for my work," he explained. "That is all. If I had talked all the week, I could not have preached on Sunday. That is all. If I had attended committee meetings, immersed myself in politics … my strength would have been consumed. That is all."[30] Campbell Morgan, who had no seminary education and no university degree, was in his study by six o'clock every morning.[31] An early start helps, but with chores and family responsibilities, perhaps we live in a very different world.

Instead of giving up on study because the ideal is impossible, we must simply set more realistic goals. I have come to realize the value of a number of shorter periods of study. I doubt if any pastor is so busy that he cannot manage one hour a day for reading, in addition to his sermon preparation time and personal Bible study and prayer. Most will also find it possible to set aside one four-hour period a week for more prolonged study. This requires the discipline of blocking off these hours in one's weekly calendar and refusing to allow them to be invaded, except by an emergency. Congregations need to be taught the essential value of this time and will usually respect it when they see it bearing fruit.

I have also discovered the immense profit of a quiet day at least once a month. I became Rector of All Souls at the age of twenty-nine, much too young and inexperienced for such a responsibility. I began living from hand to mouth. Everything piled up and got on top of me and I felt crushed by the heavy administrative load. I started having the typical pastor's nightmare: dreaming that I was half-way up the pulpit steps when I realized that I had forgotten to prepare a sermon! Then I heard Rev. L. F. E. Wilkinson speak at a pastor's conference. "Take a quiet day once a month," he said. "Go away into the country, if you can, where you can be sure of being undisturbed. Stand back, look ahead, and consider where you are going. Allow yourself to be drawn up into the mind and perspective of God. Try to see things as he sees them. Relax!" I did. I went home, and immediately marked one day a month in my diary with the letter "Q" for Quiet. And as I began to enjoy these days, the intolerable burden lifted and has never returned. In fact, so valuable did these days prove that for many years I have tried to manage one a week. I use them for those items which need unhurried and uninterrupted time – long-term planning, problems I must think and pray over, difficult letters, preparation, reading and writing. These quiet days have brought immense blessing to my life and ministry.

Every church should also release its pastor for a personal retreat for at least one week a year, perhaps breaking this up into smaller chunks of two or three days. Pastors will need to use this time well, but the value to the congregation in terms of the depth and quality of their teaching will soon be seen. Even family holidays can provide some time to read, think and discuss.

What I have suggested seems to me to be an absolute minimum of time for study and general reading. Even the busiest pastors should manage this; many will achieve more. But the minimum would mount up: one hour every day; one four-hour session every week; a full day every month; a week every year. It sounds very little. It is too little! Yet everybody who tries it is surprised to discover how much reading can be done within such a disciplined framework. It adds up to nearly 600 hours a year.

Whatever habits of study we develop, it is obviously important to gather the fruits of study. "A preacher has to be like a squirrel and has to learn to collect and store matter for the future days of winter."[32] Every reader of books develops his own practice of marking, underlining or note-taking. As one gets older some means of aiding the memory become essential. I have found it helpful, while the theme of an important book is fresh in my mind, to make a brief summary of its argument. After finishing each book I also try to write out a few of its striking quotations. I file these on cards punched with two holes, so that they can be stored in a filing cabinet or fitted into a loose-leaf book. I keep two files, the one running from Genesis to Revelation, and the other from A to Z, and file each card where I think I am most likely to find it again, or at any rate least likely to lose it! This system has served me well as it is simple and flexible. I find I can fit the notes of an average sermon on four cards, and can then add other cards containing appropriate quotations or illustrations. If I were to begin my ministry again, I would adopt the same system.

For those who use computers, various electronic filing systems are available for organizing this material. Some quotations and illustrations can even be downloaded directly from the Web or other electronic sources into one's own system.

Hindrances to Study

Some pastors may claim that, being overworked and understaffed, they have no time to study. Almost always what lies behind this argument is a false concept of the pastor's task. If the pastor holds all the reins and has no concept of shared responsibility with lay leaders, then of course there is no time to study. But the New Testament describes the church as the body of Christ, in which every member has been given gifts. Pastors who have grasped this idea will be continuously on the lookout for the gifts God has given in order to encourage people to recognize, develop and exercise them. "Each of you should use whatever gift you have received to serve others, as faithful stewards of God's grace in various forms" (1 Pet 4:10). Like the apostles, pastors are called to "prayer and the ministry of the word" (Acts 6:4). We must not let anything, even very good things, keep us from those tasks. It is tragic that many conscientious people are making the mistake the apostles were avoiding. One cannot question their dedication, their enthusiasm or their commitment, but the body of Christ does not grow to maturity that way.

What else keeps us from studying? Distraction. As computers and mobile phones become our constant companions, we all too easily allow them to eat into time that should be set aside for meditation and contemplation. We can be distracted by incoming phone calls, text messages and e-mails, or simply by the limitless opportunities of the Web. Temptations lurk on the Web too, with pornography only a mouse click away. We need the discipline to switch off these devices if we are to have time alone with God.

The ultimate obstacle to study is, frankly, laziness. Was it Ralph Waldo Emerson who said that people are as lazy as they dare to be? It is true. And we pastors can be as guilty as anyone else because our work is usually unsupervised. We have few set tasks and no set times to do them, and are left to organize our own schedule. So it is possible for us to fritter our days away until our lives sink into indiscipline and our laziness becomes painfully obvious to others.

But if we look back at the great men and women of God, we shall find that their lives were disciplined, allowing much time for prayer and study. So we need constantly to repent and renew our determination to discipline our lives and our schedules. Only a constantly fresh vision of Christ and of his commission can rescue us from laziness and keep our priorities straight. Then we shall make time to read and think, and our preaching will be fresh, faithful and relevant, yet simple enough for people to understand.

5

PREPARING SERMONS

A lazy young preacher once decided not to bother preparing his sermons. He was intelligent and spoke well, and his listeners were simple people. So he managed fairly well with his unprepared sermons. To quieten his conscience he made a vow that he would always preach without preparation, putting his trust in the Holy Spirit. Everything was fine until one day, a few minutes before the morning service began, who should walk into church but the bishop, enjoying a Sunday off. The parson was embarrassed. He had managed to fool his uneducated congregation, but he was much less sure that he could fool the bishop. So he went over to welcome his unexpected visitor and, trying to ensure that the bishop would not be critical, told him of the vow he had taken. The bishop seemed to understand, and the service began. Half-way through the sermon, however, the bishop got up and walked out. After the service a scribbled note from the bishop lay on the preacher's desk: "I release you from your vow!"

Another young minister's sin was not laziness but pride. He boasted that he could prepare his Sunday sermon in the few minutes it took him to walk to the church from his manse next door. Guess what his elders did? They bought him a new manse five miles away!

Yet another preacher who did not prepare his sermons was guilty of neither laziness nor pride. His problem was super-spirituality. He placed his confidence in the Holy Spirit and when challenged by his friends he would quote the words of Jesus "Do not worry about what to say or how to say it. At that time you will be given what to say, for it will not be you speaking, but the Spirit of your Father speaking through you" (Matt 10:19, 20). Unfortunately, he had failed to read the preceding verses, which began "When they arrest you". Christ was not referring to speaking in church but in a law court. In such a situation, we may have no time to prepare our defence. It is then that the Holy Spirit will give us words to speak. Jesus' promise has brought great comfort to prisoners without a lawyer to defend them; it offers no comfort to preachers who are too lazy or too proud or too spiritual to prepare their sermons.

Good preachers prepare conscientiously. They study the text, try to explain it clearly, look for examples and apply it to their listeners' situation. Their sermons may look effortless, yet behind each sermon lies a lifetime of discipline and hard work.

How, then, should we prepare? There is no one answer, for there is no one way to prepare sermons. Every preacher has to work out a method that suits their personality and situation. It is a mistake to copy others uncritically. Nevertheless, we can learn from one another. So here is my approach to the various steps involved in sermon preparation.

Choosing a Text

How do we decide what text to preach on? If we are regular Bible students and are keeping notes of our study, our memory becomes like a well-stocked larder with biblical texts lined up, waiting to be preached on. Four factors will help us to choose between them.

The first is the *liturgy*. Some churches follow a calendar centred round the three main Christian festivals – Advent, Easter and Pentecost. Set readings are used to prepare the listeners for these festivals, to recount the events and to consider their implications. Every year the calendar retells the story of the biblical revelation. It reminds the church how God gradually revealed himself as Creator and Father, as Son of God made flesh, and then in the person and work of the Holy Spirit. Since the set readings are appropriate, the preacher may sometimes, even often, take his text from one of them. However, it is not necessary to follow these slavishly. They are simply pointers to the day's theme and may be useful even to those whose churches do not follow the calendar. As James Stewart says:

The great landmarks of the Christian year – Advent, Christmas, Lent, Good Friday, Easter, Whitsunday [Pentecost], Trinity – set us our course, and suggest our basic themes. They compel us to keep close to the fundamental doctrines of the faith. They summon us back from the bypaths where we might be prone to linger, to the great highway of redemption. They ensure that in our preaching we shall constantly be returning to those mighty acts of God which the church exists to declare.[33]

Secondly, we need to consider *external events,* whether some national event (e.g. an election or scandal), some public debate (e.g. on capital punishment, unemployment or divorce), a natural disaster (e.g. a flood, famine or earthquake) or some other catastrophe (e.g. a plane or train crash). When people come to church, they cannot simply shut matters like these out of their minds. They bring these anxieties with them to worship and are asking "Is there any word from the Lord?" and "How should Christian people react to such things?" Preachers need to be sensitive to the big public questions in people's minds.

Thirdly, there is the *pastoral* factor – some need we notice in our congregation's spiritual pilgrimage. It is rightly said that the best preachers are always good pastors, for then they know the needs and problems, doubts, fears and hopes of their people. It is appropriate to ask the congregation what parts of Scripture they are keen to understand better and what issues in life they want the Scriptures to make clear. Lay leaders and other ministry team leaders should be encouraged to suggest topics or sermon series. There are many possible themes: doctrinal courses (e.g. the character of God), practical series (e.g. discipleship, the Ten Commandments), topical issues (e.g. guidance, prayer) and preaching through books of the Bible – chapter by chapter, paragraph by paragraph, or even verse by verse for shorter passages.

The fourth factor is *personal.* The best sermons we ever preach to others are those we have first preached to ourselves. When God himself speaks to us through a text of Scripture and it becomes clear and helpful to us, we feel compelled to share the insight and blessing. This does not mean that every sermon has to arise from our personal experience. Some of us preach on marriage while remaining unmarried, or on divorce while remaining married, and all of us have to preach on death before we have died! Yet sermons arising from deep personal conviction have a richness that James Stalker called "the blood-streak of experience". He added that "truth is doubly and trebly true when it comes from a man who speaks as if he had learned it by his own work and suffering."[34] We should keep a notebook handy so that when the light comes on and we see something clearly, we can capture the thought.

On the basis of these four factors, we can then select a single unit of thought – never less than a verse, though usually a paragraph or more. Since God gave us Scripture in books, the best long-term strategy would be to preach the units of thought in a biblical book consecutively so that the truths and the aim of the book are expounded in context and our reasoning can reflect that of the biblical author.

Studying the Text

We are now ready for the second stage of preparation. This takes time, so we should start early. The sooner we choose our text, the longer we have to mine its riches. This involves reading it over and over. Dietrich Bonhoeffer would consider it every day and "try to sink deeply into it, so as really to hear what it is saying".[35]

It is very important that we determine what the text meant when it was first spoken or written. E. D. Hirsch is right to emphasize that "a text means what its author meant".[36] We must thus discipline ourselves to think about the text's historical, geographical and cultural setting as well as its words and images. We should stop at every word and phrase and check how these are connected. We must distinguish between generalizations and the specific examples given to clarify them. We must notice the genre, that is, the type of writing style. Poetry such as is found in the psalms and in much prophetic material uses different techniques to historical accounts or letters. In a poem we find images and vivid words packed together to inspire as well as to teach.

This type of detailed study, taking notes of all we see, is very important before we try to isolate the dominant thought that we will be preaching on. You may find the following six questions helpful as you tackle this task and work to crystallize what you have seen. They will help you to remain faithful to the content and intent of the biblical text:

1. What is the function of the text in its context? Is it a command, an example, an explanation, a promise, or some combination of these? This question is extremely important since we want the sermon to reflect what the text is doing, not just what it is saying.

2. What is the main thing the author is talking about? What word or phrase best captures the subject of the verse?

3. What is the author saying about this subject? Everything in the rest of the text must relate in some way to the main issue.

4. What response does the Holy Spirit want to this text? Our answer to the first question will give us a clue. If the section is a command, then obedience is required; we just need to determine what that obedience involves. If the text is an explanation, it should bring understanding that can lead to faith. We must take care not to base our answer to this question on mere guesswork or our own experience. We must allow the text and its context to explain how the Holy Spirit wants us to respond.

5. How does *this* text evoke this response? For instance, does the author present arguments (as Paul does in Romans) or create a word picture (as in Psalm 23)? The best preachers use their answer to this question as the key as to how to influence their listeners to respond. They let the text do what the text wants to do!

6. How does this text fit into the history of salvation, the broader drama of redemption? We must understand how our text contributes to the story line of the Bible and, therefore, how it points to Christ.

When we get accurate answers to these questions we shall have removed at least some of the obstacles to faithful preaching. If we capture what the text is saying and doing, we will know what the passage is talking about, what it is saying about that subject, what response it actually calls for, how it stirs up that response and what it contributes to the larger picture of God's saving work. If, on the other hand, we do not notice these things, we are likely to preach merely what comes to our minds, what happens to occur to us when we read the passage, instead of what the text is designed by God to say and do.

Meditating on the Text

Next we must take time to meditate on our text, to think carefully about it until it touches and moves us. We should turn it over and over in our minds, like Mary the mother of Jesus who treasured all the things the shepherds told her and "pondered them in her heart" (Luke 2:18, 19). We should extract the sweetness like a bee with a blossom; gnaw it like a dog with a bone; suck it as a child sucks an orange; and chew it as a cow chews its cud.

All this time we should be praying, crying humbly to God for light from the Spirit of truth. Like Moses, we must beg him to show us his glory (Exod 33:18). Study is no substitute for prayer; prayer is no substitute for study. We must do both. It may help to study on our knees, because this attitude reminds us that we worship the God who reveals himself in the Bible, and we are humble before him. In Daniel 9 we find an excellent example of this. Study of the Scriptures (9:2) led to a humble prayer of confession and petition (9:3–19). The Lord heard and gave Daniel greater understanding (9:20–23).

As we meditate prayerfully, we should write down our insights and further questions. Sometimes there will be a flash of insight. Don't lose it! It will help you to convey the meaning of the passage to your listeners.

There is no substitute for individual study, but that does not mean that we cannot get help from others. We can get valuable insights from commentaries. There is also value in inviting a group – a ministry team, small group leaders or other pastors – to look at the text with us. They may well see things that our eyes miss.

We can also benefit from using our computers as we study. Bible software programs offer access to older commentaries and facilitate word searches that would have taken many hours just a few years ago. The Internet enables us to do research so easily that factual errors in our sermons are almost inexcusable.

But computers offer temptations as well as opportunities. Our own study and application of the text can be short-circuited if we simply download and preach someone else's sermon, using their illustrations and ideas. Such plagiarism, or stealing of sermons, is at least as old as Jeremiah's time (Jer 23:30), but it is still immoral. Moreover preachers may be tempted to draw dubious analogies using only half-understood information. Or they may try to cultivate an image as someone who is extremely knowledgeable – which may be neither true nor desirable.

There is no quick substitute for sustained, personal reflection on the text.

Isolating the Dominant Thought

As we continue to meditate through reading, prayer and study, we should be searching for the dominant idea in our text. Every text has a main thought, a big idea, a main thrust. We should persevere in meditation until it emerges and becomes clear. This is necessary because "every sermon should be ruthlessly unitary in its theme."[37]

If, as we argued in chapter three, God speaks through what he has spoken, then it is essential to ask ourselves "What is he saying?" and "Where does his emphasis lie?" True, there may be several acceptable ways of handling a text and several different lessons to learn from it. For example, it would be permissible to use the parable of the Good Samaritan to teach that love expresses itself in sacrificial service. Yet the main thrust of Jesus' story is the shocking fact that a despised Samaritan outsider did what two religious Jews were unwilling to do. It is not possible to discuss the parable accurately without stressing this racial point and its implied criticism of all religion that, however strict, is false because it is loveless. Every text has an overriding thrust. We must have the integrity to discover this and resist the temptation to give the text a twist or stress of our own.

A sermon, unlike a lecture, should convey only one major message. Students are expected to take notes because lecturers provide so much information during the class. A sermon, however, is quite different. As a living word from God to his people, it should make its impact on them then and there. They will not remember the details. We should not expect them to do so. But they should remember the dominant thought, because all the sermon's details have been structured to help them grasp its message, feel its power, and respond.

> No sermon is ready for preaching ... until we can express its theme in a short, pregnant sentence as clear as a crystal. I find the getting of that sentence is the hardest, the most exacting and the most fruitful labour in my study ... I do not think any sermon ought to be preached, or even written, until that sentence has emerged, clear and lucid as a cloudless moon.[38]

Ideally the whole service should be built around this theme. The early part of the service should begin to draw the minds and hearts of the congregation towards the biblical theme and to prepare them to receive it. The opening hymns and worship songs, as well as the intercessionary prayer, may be more general, but the Bible readings should be relevant. So should the spiritual song or hymn before the sermon. And the song or hymn after the sermon should help us to express our response. We should not be afraid of such repetition.

In our sermon preparation, we must not bypass the discipline of waiting patiently for the dominant thought to reveal itself. We have to be ready to pray and think ourselves deep into the text, until we become its humble and obedient servant. Then there will be no danger of text-twisting. Instead, the word of God will dominate our mind, set fire to our hearts, and control the development of our sermon. Then his word will make a lasting impression on the congregation.

Arranging the Material

So far we have gathered many ideas about the text and tried to isolate its dominant thought. Now we have to organize our ideas so that they all point to that thought. We are not trying to produce a masterpiece; we are trying to ensure that the main idea of the text will have maximum impact, accomplishing the same thing in our listeners that it set out to do in the lives of its first hearers (or readers).

The first step in doing this is to *discard irrelevant thoughts*. This is easier said than done. During our hours of meditation, many blessed thoughts and wonderful ideas may have occurred to us. It is tempting to drag them all in somehow. Do not give in to the temptation! Irrelevant material will weaken the sermon's effect and those other ideas will be useful some other time. We need the strength of mind to keep them until then. Positively, we have to shape our material to our theme so that our main idea stands out boldly. In order to do this, we need a structure, words and illustrations.

The second step is to *organize our thoughts into a structure.* An unstructured sermon is like a jellyfish, all flesh and no bones. However, a sermon whose structure is too noticeable is like a skeleton, all bones and no flesh. Neither jellyfish nor skeletons make good sermons!

The structure of a sermon is too visible when it is too clever (e.g. every point starts with the same letter of the alphabet) or too complicated (e.g. a sermon by Richard Baxter that had sixty-five points!).[39] Outlines which advertise themselves like this are always distracting. The purpose of the outline, like the purpose of the skeleton, is to support the body while keeping itself largely out of sight.

This is not to say that pastors should never disclose the structure of their sermon to their listeners. Sometimes it can be helpful to do this, either verbally or by projecting it on a screen. But the structure should be simple and the visual representation of it should only be an aid. It is all too easy for PowerPoint slides to block person-to-person communication because the congregation look at the screen and not at the preacher.

A second danger to watch out for is an unnatural structure. Some preachers force an outline on their text, muddying the clear waters of truth and confusing the listeners. The golden rule for sermon outlines is that each text must be allowed to supply its own structure. The skilful expositor allows the text to open itself up before our eyes, like a rose unfolding to the morning sun and displaying its previously hidden beauty. Dr. Alexander McLaren, for example, was said to be able to touch the text "with a silver hammer, and it immediately broke up into natural and memorable divisions".[40] Spurgeon uses the same image, saying that after much labour one will at last find a text that "sparkles as it falls in pieces and you perceive jewels of the rarest radiance flashing from within".[41]

There are many ways of structuring a sermon, and different texts demand different treatment. We need to practise different techniques and not get stuck on a single method. For example, sometimes we may start with the big idea and then draw out particular conclusions, anchoring each part of our exposition in the text. On other occasions, we will develop the main theme slowly, dealing with individual points and only at the end indicating what everything adds up to. This method is especially useful when we are dealing with narratives. The climax of a story usually comes at the end, and we would be foolish to tell it at the beginning. Often, however, we can combine these methods.

Once we have the structure clear in our minds, we need to *flesh it out with words*. It is impossible to convey a precise message without choosing precise words. We should be like the Preacher in Ecclesiastes who "searched to find just the right words, and what he wrote was upright and true". Such words are "like goads" that prick the conscience and stimulate the mind; they are "like firmly embedded nails" because they stick in the memory and are not easily dislodged (Eccl 12:10, 11). So it is worth taking trouble over our words.

The words we choose should be as simple and clear as possible, and should be used in short sentences. Moreover, they should be vivid, painting pictures in the minds of our listeners.

C. S. Lewis gave common-sense advice on this topic when he advised writers to

- Be clear and avoid any possible ambiguity.
- Prefer simple words to long ones designed only to impress.
- Use concrete nouns rather than abstract ones.
- Show, don't tell. In other words,

   Don't use adjectives which merely tell us how you want us to feel about the thing you are describing. I mean, instead of telling us a thing was "terrible", describe it so that we'll be terrified. Don't say it was "delightful"; make us say "delightful" when we've read the description. You see, all those words (horrifying, wonderful, hideous, exquisite) are only saying to your readers "please will you do my job for me".

- Don't exaggerate. If you use "infinitely" when you mean "very", "you'll have no word left when you want to talk about something *really* infinite".[42]

So, we must search for simple words which our listeners will understand, vivid words which will help them to picture what we are saying, and honest words which tell the plain truth without exaggeration.

Remember in all this that words have meaning only in context. Choose the right word, but don't assume that posting it next to a bullet point on your PowerPoint will adequately communicate your idea.

What we put in words we must always *supplement with images or illustrations.* The word "illustrate" means to illuminate, to throw light on a dark object, and this is what our sermon illustrations should do. People find it very difficult to handle abstract ideas; we need to convert them either into symbols (as in mathematics) or into pictures. It has been well said that a picture is worth a thousand words.

Do you remember that Paul reminded the Galatians that "Before your very eyes Jesus Christ was clearly portrayed as crucified" (Gal 3:1). The crucifixion had taken place some twenty years previously, and none of Paul's Galatian readers had witnessed it. Yet by his vivid preaching Paul had been able to bring this event out of the past into the present, as a dramatic visual image. This is the purpose of every illustration: to stimulate people's imagination and to help them to see things clearly in their minds. Illustrations transform the abstract into the concrete, the ancient into the present, the unfamiliar into the familiar, the general into the particular, the vague into the precise, the unreal into the real, and the invisible into the visible. A good speaker "turns his hearers' ears into eyes, and makes them see what he speaks of".[43]

Not surprisingly, one of the most important elements in coming up with good illustrations is imagination, that is, the ability to imagine "invisible things, and ... to present them as though they were visible to others".[44]

There are four dangers, however, that we must watch out for. The first is that illustrations can be too prominent, thrusting themselves into the spotlight instead of shining light on something difficult to understand. This kind of illustration is remembered for itself long after the truth which it was illustrating has been forgotten. This danger is particularly acute when we use technology to incorporate film clips into sermons. It can be difficult to recapture the listeners' attention, and so before using a clip, we need to think about whether it is appropriate and tasteful, whether it requires an explanation, and whether it will transport the viewers into a world of fantasy rather than lead them towards reality.

The second danger is that the analogy may be inappropriate. We have to make clear what part of the likeness is important. For example, when

Jesus told us to become like little children, he did not mean that we are to be childlike in every respect. He was not recommending childish immaturity, naughtiness, irresponsibility, innocence or ignorance. He was focusing on a child's humility – children know that they cannot cope on their own. In the same way, we are as dependent on grace, as children are on their parents. There are other biblical passages in which we are told not to be like children (Jer 1:7; 1 Cor 3:1, 2; 14:20; Heb 5:11–14). So it is always dangerous, and often misleading, to build too much on an analogy. It is wrong to suggest that, because two objects or events are similar in one way, they must be totally the same.

The third danger is the temptation to use too many or too few illustrations. "A sermon that is entirely without pictures, without illustrations, is likely to reach only those whose intellectual discipline makes it possible for them to appreciate abstractions." On the other hand, "a sermon with too many illustrations is like a woman with too many jewels, and the jewels which are originally intended to enhance the figure, hide it".[45]

Finally, we must take great care about how we present illustrations. If we are careless and have the facts wrong, or claim a story as our own when it came from another source, over-generalize from the story, or play to the listeners by gratuitous use of humour or manipulate them with emotionally wrenching stories, we may find that we lose our credibility with careful listeners. We cannot afford this.

Where do we find illustrations? One good source is the Bible. It is packed with illustrations. Think of the Old Testament. "As a father has compassion on his children, so the Lord has compassion on those who fear him" (Ps 103:13). "The wicked ... are like the chaff that the wind blows away" (Ps 1:4). "I will be like the dew to Israel; he will blossom like a lily. Like a cedar of Lebanon he will send down his roots" (Hos 14:5). "They will soar on wings like eagles" (Isa 40:31). "Is not my word like fire ... and like a hammer that breaks a rock in pieces?" (Jer 23:29). Or take the New Testament. "You are the salt of the earth. ... You are the light of the world" (Matt 5:13, 14). "The Son of Man in his day will be like the lightning which flashes and lights up the sky from one end to the other" (Luke 17:24). "Woe to you, teachers of the law and Pharisees, you hypocrites! You are like whitewashed tombs, which look beautiful on the outside but on the inside are full of the bones of the dead" (Matt 23:27). "Just as a nursing mother cares for her children, so we cared for you" (1 Thess 2:7, 8). "What is your life? You are a mist that appears for a little while and then vanishes" (Jas 4:14). Then there are the parables that Jesus told. Our list could be much longer.

Some preachers have great skill in retelling biblical stories and parables in modern language, while others are able to invent fresh, modern parables. The most effective illustrations, however, are probably stories from history or biography, from current affairs or our own experience. Then the biblical truth connects with the widest possible circumstances.

It is also important to remember that some illustrations may be no more than a word or a phrase that conveys a dramatic picture. When we talk of God "breaking through our defences", people can visualize defending themselves against attacks. When we say that the Holy Spirit is "prying open" our closed minds to new truth, our listeners can almost hear the creaking of the box lid as it reluctantly opens under the pressure of the hammer or screwdriver.

Every preacher must be constantly on the lookout for illustrations. Not that we read books and listen to people only to collect sermon material! Yet we would be wise to write down ideas which come to us, as well as the best quotations from every book we read.

Adding the Conclusion

Only after preparing the body of the sermon, are we ready to write our introduction and conclusion. Strangely enough, the conclusion should be written before the introduction, for in writing the conclusion we bring the message to its final focus and application. Only after doing this, will we be sufficiently clear about what we are introducing.

Some of us seem incapable of concluding anything, let alone our sermons! We circle around, like a plane without instruments on a foggy day, unable to land. Others of us stop too abruptly. Our sermons are like a play without a finale, like music without a crescendo or climax. So it is worth looking at the conclusion in more detail.

The first task of the *conclusion* is to sum up, to repeat the main ideas of the sermon. We should not be afraid to repeat ourselves. "It is no trouble for me to write the same things to you again," said Paul, "and it is a safeguard for you" (Phil 3:1). Peter was of the same opinion: "I will always remind you of these things, even though you know them ... I think it is right to refresh your memory as long as I live (2 Pet 1:12, 13). Some skilful carpenters can drive a nail in with one mighty blow; most find it safer to hammer it in with several blows. Just so, our listeners need the truth to be driven home by the hammer-blows of repetition. But we should guard against mere repetition; we have to find a different way to make our point.

A conclusion also requires personal application. Our expectation as the sermon comes to an end is not merely that people will understand or remember or enjoy our teaching, but that they will respond to it. Not that this response should come only at the end, for we should be applying the truths as we go along. But it is a mistake to reveal our conclusion too soon in case we lose our listeners' sense of expectation. It is better to keep something back. At the end then, by the Holy Spirit's power, we can urge our listeners to take action or do whatever the text calls them to do.

The biblical authors were quite clear that this was the purpose of their teaching. Ezekiel was appointed as "a watchman for the house of Israel" in order to warn them of God's judgment and to call them to repentance. The great pain of his prophetic ministry was that the people refused to respond. God said to him, "You are nothing more than one who sings love songs with a beautiful voice and plays an instrument well, for they hear your words, but do not put them into practice" (Ezek 3: 17; 33:30–32). Listening to sermons and listening to concerts should be two very different experiences: music is to be enjoyed; Scripture is to be obeyed. Jesus told his disciples, "Now that you know these things, you will be blessed if you do them" (John 13:17; see also John 3:18–21). The apostles make it plain that truth brings with it moral demands: it is to be obeyed, not merely heard or believed (Rom 1:18–23; 2 Thess 2:10–12; James 1:22–25; 1 John 1:6, 8; 2 John 4, 6; 3 John 3, 4).

How we apply our sermon depends on our text and our congregation. We meditated on our text until it yielded its main idea. This is the idea we want our listeners to feel and to go away determined to act on. Does the text call for repentance or increase our faith? Does it encourage worship, demand obedience, call on us to witness, or challenge us to serve? The text itself determines the response we long for.

As for our congregation, we have already emphasized the need to know them and their spiritual condition. Richard Bernard writing in 1607 listed some of what the preacher should hope to do:

> Inform the ignorant, confirm such as have understanding, reclaim the vicious, encourage the virtuous, convince the erroneous, strengthen the weak, recover again the backslider, resolve those that doubt, feed with milk and strong meat continually, in season and out of season.[46]

The only way to do this is to use our God-given imagination to picture our congregation, and relate their lives to the text we have been studying. Susan's husband has recently died. She is experiencing the shock of bereavement and loneliness: what has my text to say to her? Or to Angela, who has never come to terms with her singleness? Or to Samuel, who is feeling the weight of new responsibilities following his promotion? Or to John and Mary, who have just got married and are setting up their home? Or to those students facing final exams and wondering about their careers? Or to that Thomas who is full of doubts, that Agrippa who is still thinking about the gospel, or that Paul who is newly committed to Christ? It is good to let our mind wander over the church family and ask prayerfully what message God might have for each one from our text. George Whitefield practised this by actually naming the sort of people he knew were listening to his preaching:

> I know that many of you come here out of curiosity: though you come only to see the congregation, yet if you come to Jesus Christ, Christ will accept of you. Are there any cursing, swearing soldiers here? Will you come to Christ, and list yourselves under the banner of the dear Redeemer? You are all welcome to Christ. Are there any little boys or little girls here? Come to Christ, and he will erect his kingdom in you … you that are old and gray headed, come to Jesus Christ, and you shall be kings and priests to your God … If there be any of you ambitious of honour, do you want a crown, a sceptre? Come

to Christ, and the Lord Jesus Christ will give you a kingdom
that no man shall take from you.[47]

To give another example, a young man invited to preach on "You shall
not commit adultery" gave a sermon that was biblical, brave, direct
and practical. He ended with four applications: single young people
should keep themselves pure for their future partner and learn to be
strong when temptation comes; people in an adulterous relationship
should break it off, despite the pain; married people should work at their
marriage and set an example to the many young people who come from
broken homes and have no role models; and the local church should
have the courage to accuse and discipline offenders, in obedience to
Jesus' teaching in Matthew 18:15–17.[48]

We need also to be aware that people hear sermons through
different filters. Some will be open to our message. Others will resist
it because they see it as a threat to their world view, or culture, or
family unity, or self-worth, or sinful way of life, or economic lifestyle.
If we are aware of this resistance, we may need to be like the apostles
and resort to persuasion in the conclusion (Acts 17:4; 18:4; 19:8; 2
Cor 5:11). We may seek to persuade by argument as we anticipate and
answer people's objections, or by warning them of the consequences
of disobedience. We may need to work indirectly, first arousing a
moral judgment in them and then turning it upon themselves, as
Nathan did with David. We may need to plead, applying the gentle
pressure of God's love.

Then, as the sermon ends, it is good to invite the people to pray.
Sometimes we will pray aloud, seeking to express the congregation's
response to God's word. At other times it may be wiser to call the people
to silent prayer. The Holy Spirit may be prompting different responses
in different hearts, which a single prayer could never cover.

Planning the Introduction

Now that we are clear about where our sermon will end, we can work on
our *introduction*. If this is too long, it will distract from the sermon itself,
but the more common mistake is to shorten it too much, or even to do

away with it altogether, in order to jump into the subject immediately. This is unwise.

A good introduction serves at least three purposes. First, it awakes interest, stimulates curiosity, and makes us long to know God's perspective on this matter. Secondly, it enables the listeners to sense that they are listening to someone who is qualified to speak for God from this text. If the preacher is living a godly life before the congregation and has spoken truthfully and accurately in the past, they may already know this, but it cannot be taken for granted. We must stand before them as faithful servants of the word whose aim, like Paul, is that "the message of the Lord may spread rapidly and be honoured" in the lives of our listeners (2 Thess 3:1). Thirdly, it introduces the dominant idea and leads the hearers into it. It is reasonably easy to construct introductions which fulfil one of these functions. But we need to do all three – and without using too many words!

The first aim is achieved by using an example, a quotation, a question or an event to bring the message into focus. The second is achieved by prayer, asking God to help us avoid anything – no matter how trivial – that would disqualify us as stewards of God's word. The third is achieved by avoiding any introductory story, quotation, question or thought that does not directly prepare listeners to hear the message of the text before us.

Some preachers simply announce and read their text, but people may see this as very traditional and very dull. Most of the time, we would be wise to begin with a situation relating to the topic the text discusses, instead of the text itself. I remember, for example, conducting a pastors' seminar in Guatemala City soon after a terrible earthquake had killed 23,000 people and left more than a million homeless. Would it have been appropriate for the local preachers to start their sermon that Sunday with, "My text this morning is ..."? Would it not have been more natural to begin: "We meet this morning in great sorrow. Many of us have lost a relative or friend. Others have lost their home and possessions. Why does God allow such disasters? That is the question in all our hearts and minds. How can we still believe in a God of love?" If we then announced and read a text that related directly to the problem of God's provision or the assurance of his love, we would be more likely to keep the congregation's attention. We need to start where the people are, rather than where we hope to take them.

Writing Out the Message and Praying Over It

The question now arises as to whether to write the sermon out. Since God has made us all different and given us distinct personalities and talents, there can be no fixed rule for everybody. Nevertheless, there seems to be agreement that we should avoid two extremes. The first is complete improvisation. Few people are such clear thinkers and talkers that they can express themselves well without written preparation. Charles Simeon advised his students not to preach without notes until they had preached 300 to 400 written sermons.[49]

The opposite extreme is slavery to our notes so that we read a sermon word for word. Jonathan Edwards, for example, "wrote his sermons; and in so fine and so illegible a hand, that they could be read only by being brought near to the eye. He carried his notes with him into the desk, and read most that he wrote: still, he was not confined to them."[50] While God's blessing rested on him, this approach will not work in our generation, which demands face-to-face interaction between the preacher and congregation.

There seems to be only one way to combine careful use of language with person-to-person contact: we must write the sermon in our study, but must not merely read it from the pulpit. This writing is a most worthwhile discipline. First, it ensures that we think clearly. Wordy preachers can hide careless thinking with clever speech; it is much more difficult to get away with a cover-up on paper. In fact, it is impossible if we are honest. Secondly, writing helps us to avoid using the same old phrases over and over again. It challenges us to develop new ways of expressing old truths.

These days, it may be tempting to replace writing the sermon with cutting and pasting material from the Web. While we can use the Web to check the accuracy of illustrations, we still need to take the time to draft our own sermon. The physical act of writing or typing will help us to remember what we want to say and will encourage us to adapt what we have read to the congregation to which we are to preach.

Once we have written out the sermon, we should not try to memorize it so that we can recite it in the pulpit. This would require far too much time and work, and there is a real danger that we might forget our lines. What is more, we would have to concentrate far more on remembering, than on our message and congregation.

One use of the written sermon that lies between memorizing it or reading it is illustrated by Joseph Pilmore:

> He wrote his sermons, and ... his manuscript was always before him. He began not only by reading, but by reading very deliberately, and with little animation; but he would gradually wax warm, and you would see his eyes begin to kindle, and the muscles of his face to move and expand, until at length his soul would be all on fire, and he would be rushing onward extemporaneously almost with the fury of a cataract. And the only use he would make of his manuscript in such cases would be to roll it up in his hand, and literally shake it at his audience.[51]

A better alternative is to rewrite the sermon in note form, and to take these notes into the pulpit with us. If we have prepared carefully and written out the sermon and prayed over it, much of it will come back to our minds easily when we are preaching. At the same time, we will have a certain amount of freedom to depart from our notes or to elaborate on them. Professor James Stewart, a wonderfully fluent preacher, told me that this was his method: "I did try always to write the morning sermon at least out in full. ... On the Saturday morning I would reduce this to a one- or two-page summary, which then accompanied me to church on the Sunday."[52]

After the writing comes the praying. Of course we prayed before we began to prepare, and we have tried to continue in an attitude of prayer throughout our preparation. But now that the sermon is finished and written, we need to pray over it. I recommend that we do this before leaving for church on Sunday. It is on our knees before the Lord that we can make the message our own, possess or repossess it until it possesses us. Then, when we preach it, it will come neither from our notes, nor from our memory, but out of the depths of our personal faith, as a genuine cry from our heart. As Baxter wrote, "a minister should take some special pains with his heart before he is to go to the congregation".[53] Every preacher knows the difference between a heavy sermon which trundles along the runway like an overloaded passenger jet and never gets airborne, and a sermon which has "what a bird has, a sense of direction and wings".[54]

The prophets and wise men spoke of this in the olden days. Jeremiah said "But if I say, 'I will not mention his word or speak any more in his name', his word is in my heart like a fire, a fire shut up in my bones. I am weary of holding it in; indeed I cannot" (Jer 20:9). Job's younger "comforter", Elihu, angry because the first three speakers had found no answer to Job's situation, had a similar experience: "I am full of words, and the spirit within me compels me; inside I am like bottled-up wine, like new wineskins ready to burst. I must speak and find relief" (Job 32:18–20). The psalmist, oppressed by the wicked around him, said, "My heart grew hot within me. While I meditated, the fire burned; then I spoke with my tongue (Ps 39:3). God's message within us should be like burning fire or fermenting wine. The pressure should begin to build inside us, until we feel we can contain it no longer. It is then that we are ready to preach.

The whole process of sermon preparation, from beginning to end, was excellently summed up by an African American preacher who said, "First, I reads myself full, next I thinks myself clear, next I prays myself hot, and then I lets go."

How Long Does It Take?

Students and young preachers want to know how long it takes to prepare a sermon. It is impossible to give a simple reply. The best answer is "your whole life!" In a way, every sermon is influenced by everything we have ever learned, and is a reflection of the kind of person we have become over the years. The reason it is difficult to calculate the actual hours is because no-one can say precisely when the process begins. Shall we include the time spent in background reading? After we have been studying and preparing for a few years, we never come to a verse or passage which we have not read or thought about before. So we come to it with the ideas we have gathered over time.

However, as a rough guideline, I think that beginners will need ten to twelve hours from the moment the text is chosen to the moment the sermon is written out. Experienced preachers are not likely to reduce this to less than five to six hours. On average, one needs at least one hour's preparation for every five minutes preached.

6

SINCERITY AND EARNESTNESS

Nothing sickens people more than deceit or hypocrisy; nothing is more attractive than sincerity. People expect high standards of honesty from preachers and sniff around like dogs after a rat to see if they can discover any contradictions in us. We are personally committed to our message and must be sincere. Christ himself condemned hypocrites harshly.

There are two sides to this sincerity: preachers must mean what they say in the pulpit, and must practice what they preach when out of it. As Richard Baxter put it, "he that means as he speaks will surely do as he speaks".[55]

The very first requirement is that those who proclaim the gospel must themselves have received the gospel; those who preach Christ must know Christ. Spurgeon describes an unconverted preacher as follows.

> A graceless pastor is a blind man elected to a professorship of optics, philosophizing upon light and vision ... while he himself is absolutely in the dark! He is a dumb man elevated to the chair of music; a deaf man fluent upon symphonies and harmonies! He is a mole professing to educate eaglets; a limpet elected to preside over angels.[56]

We smile at his descriptions, yet such people have been found in the pulpits of some churches. Rev. William Haslam, for example, was a diligent minister in the Church of England from 1842. But he was not satisfied, having no spring of living water within him. Nine years after his ordination, he preached on the text, "What think ye of Christ?" As he was preaching, the Holy Spirit (probably in answer to many prayers) opened his eyes to see the Christ he was speaking about, and his heart to believe in him. The change in Haslam was so obvious that a local preacher, who happened to be there, jumped up and shouted, "The parson is converted! Hallelujah!" His voice was drowned by the praises of the congregation. Haslam "joined in the outburst of praise, and, to make it more orderly ... gave out the doxology ... and the people sang it with heart and voice, over and over again." The news spread like wildfire "that the parson was converted, and that by his own sermon, in his own pulpit!" His conversion was the beginning of a great revival in his district, with a vivid sense of God's presence, and conversions almost daily for the next three years. In later years God called him into the most unusual ministry of leading many of his fellow ministers to a personal knowledge of Jesus Christ.[57]

Church members have a right to expect that the Holy Spirit has done more than just convert their pastors. They look for the fruit of the Spirit as well, for Christian maturity. Paul told Timothy and Titus to be models of Christian behaviour (1 Tim 4:12; Titus 2:7). Peter similarly instructed the elders to set an example (1 Pet 5:3). The emphasis is plain. "A man cannot only preach, he must also live. And the life that he lives ... is one of two things: either it emasculates his preaching or it gives it flesh and blood."[58] We cannot hide what we are. Indeed, what we are speaks as plainly as what we say. When these two voices blend, the impact of the message is doubled. But when they contradict each other, the positive witness is cancelled by the other.

This leads to a practical problem. The congregation tend to see preachers as models of Christian maturity, to put us on a pedestal, and to idealize, even idolize, us. We know, however, that this is at least partly false. Although the grace of God has been and continues to be at work in us, we are not as perfect as they seem to think. So what should we do? Does sincerity demand that we destroy this fairy story and tell the truth about ourselves from the pulpit?

As always we should avoid extreme reactions. To turn the pulpit into a confessional is not appropriate or helpful. Yet, to pretend to be perfect is dishonest and discouraging to the congregation. So we should admit the truth. Like them, we are weak and sinful, exposed to temptation and suffering. Like them, we struggle with doubt, fear and sin. Like them, we depend continuously on God's forgiving and liberating grace.

In this way the preacher remains a model – but a model of humbleness and truth.

The New Testament emphasizes the need for the preacher to be self-disciplined. "Keep watch over yourselves" Paul reminded the elders of the Ephesian church, adding "and all the flock of which the Holy Spirit has made you overseers" (Acts 20:28). He wrote to Timothy: "Watch your life and doctrine closely" (1 Tim 4:16). The order in these statements is important. Pastors have God-given responsibilities both to the congregation we serve and to the doctrine we teach. Yet our first responsibility is to guard our personal walk with God and our loyalty to him. Nobody can be a good pastor or teacher of others who is not first a good servant of Jesus Christ.

Disciplined habits of pastoral visiting, counselling, theological study and sermon preparation become barren unless they are supported by disciplined personal devotion, especially biblical meditation and prayer. Every pastor knows how difficult this is. We may be misunderstood and opposed; we may become lonely and discouraged; we shall certainly grow weary in mind and body. Even the strongest personalities collapse under these pressures, unless the power of God is being revealed in our weakness and the life of Jesus in our mortal body. Then "inwardly we are being renewed day by day" (2 Cor 4:7–11, 16).

The Importance of Sincerity

It is very easy to slip from strict honesty into pretence or hypocrisy, so we need to remind ourselves why sincerity is important. The New Testament gives at least three reasons.

First, it warns us that although teaching is a spiritual gift and a great privilege, it brings with it many dangers. Paul suggests to the Jewish leaders, "If you are convinced that you are a guide for the blind, a light for those who are in the dark, an instructor of the foolish, a teacher of infants, because you have in the law the embodiment of knowledge and truth – you, then, who teach others, do you not teach yourself?" (Rom 2:17–21). Hypocrisy in teachers is unacceptable because they should know better! Teachers cannot argue that they do not know their own curriculum! Jesus judged the Pharisees harshly, because "they do not practise what they teach" (Matt 23:1–3). This is why James gave the surprising advice: "Not many of you should presume to be teachers, my brothers and sisters, because you know that we who teach will be judged more strictly" (Jas 3:1).

Secondly, hypocrisy causes great offence. Many people have separated themselves from Christ because of the hypocritical behaviour of some who claim to follow him. Paul knew this, and was determined not to be an obstacle to other people's faith: "We put no stumbling block in anyone's path, so that our ministry will not be discredited. Rather, as servants of God we commend ourselves in every way" (2 Cor 6:3, 4). As evidence Paul lists how he had suffered for his faith. There was no contradiction between his message and his behaviour. People will not accept our message if our life contradicts it – just as they would not buy a cold cure from a salesman who coughs and sneezes between each sentence!

The third argument for sincerity is the positive influence a "real" person can have. Paul, for instance, firmly "renounced secret and shameful ways", and committed himself to "setting forth the truth plainly" and to commending himself "to everyone's conscience in the sight of God" (2 Cor 4:2). He detested trickery and deceit, and could appeal to both God and fellow-believers as witnesses to his openness (1 Thess 2:1–12). There was nothing in his life or lifestyle that prevented his hearers from believing his message. He was believable because what he said matched what he was.

Sincere believers attract unbelievers. Even the fiercest critics of the evangelist Billy Graham respected his sincerity. Similarly, we are told that a friend once met the philosopher David Hume (who rejected Christianity) hurrying along a London street and asked him where he was going. Hume replied that he was going to hear George Whitefield preach. "But surely," his friend asked in astonishment, "you don't believe what Whitefield preaches, do you?" "No, I don't," answered Hume, "but he does."[59] Hypocrisy always repels; genuineness always attracts.

One of the chief proofs of genuineness is the willingness to suffer for what we believe. The faithfulness of the true servant of God is proved when opposition comes (2 Cor 6:4, 5). Paul even spoke of his sufferings as his credentials or qualifications (2 Cor 11:21–33; 1 Thess 2:1–4; 2 Tim 3:10–12). He was prepared to be "persecuted for the cross of Christ" (Gal 5:11; 6:12). It is often through a dark and lonely struggle that faith emerges:

> It is not from a pulpit but a cross that power-filled words are spoken. Sermons need to be seen as well as heard to be effectual. Eloquence, homiletical skill, biblical knowledge are not enough. Anguish, pain, engagement, sweat and blood punctuate the stated truths to which men will listen.[60]

Sincerity in Manner

This is probably the best context in which to mention briefly the practical matters of voice production and gesture. These should not be rehearsed, for preachers are not actors, and the pulpit is not a stage. An actor is self-conscious, whereas what is needed in the pulpit is self-forgetful sincerity. Our presentation should flow naturally from our sincere desire to let God speak through us. We should focus on cultivating a growing awareness of God and of the people to whom we are speaking. This will help us both to be ourselves and to forget ourselves!

However, it can be valuable to ask a friend to comment on our voice and mannerisms. This is what I did when I began to preach. I received feedback from two friends who were medical students (and thus trained in the art of observation).[61] Although I remember being shattered by some of what they said, their criticisms were always valuable. Colleagues can also be asked for feedback. This may sometimes be given by a group that may include members of the congregation who are not preachers. This assessment should consider the way we speak, our gestures, manner and mannerisms, as well as the content of the sermon, our use of Scripture, the clarity with which we present our dominant thought and aim, structure, words, illustrations, our introduction and conclusion. Preachers' clubs can also provide feedback, and can help us by identifying weaknesses in our preparation as well.

Earnestness

Earnestness goes one step beyond sincerity. To be sincere is to *mean* what we say and to *do* what we say; to be earnest is also to *feel* what we say. Earnestness is the deep feeling essential to preaching. "No man can be a great preacher without great feeling" wrote James W. Alexander of Princeton.[62] Elsewhere he says "it is a matter of universal observation that a speaker who would excite deep feeling must feel deeply himself".[63]

To handle issues of eternal life and death as if we were discussing the weather is inexcusable. How can we deliver a solemn message in a casual manner, or refer to the eternal destinies of men and women as if we were discussing where they will spend their summer holidays? Christians who care are earnest. They care about God, about his glory and his Christ. When Paul was in Athens, he was "distressed" because he saw the city choked with idols, he was angry about the idolatry, and defended the honour of the one, living and true God (Acts 17:16). And when he told the Philippians that many were living "as enemies of the cross of Christ", he could do so only "with tears" (3:18). The thought that people were trusting in their own righteousness instead of Christ, and that they were being self-indulgent rather than holy, made him weep.

We should also care about people in their lostness. Jesus wept over the city of Jerusalem because its inhabitants rejected his love and did not realize what was best for them (Matt 23:37; Luke 19:41, 42). For Paul preaching and weeping went hand-in-hand. For three years in Ephesus he "never stopped warning ... night and day with tears" (Acts 20:31; compare vv. 19, 37). And weeping did not die out with the New Testament. Christian evangelists, bringing the good news of salvation but fearing that some might reject it and thereby condemn themselves to hell, have never been far from tears. D. L. Moody "could never speak of a lost soul without tears in his eyes".[64] When George Whitefield preached, people always realized that he loved them:

> His tears – and he could seldom manage a sermon without weeping – were totally unaffected. "You blame me for weeping," he would say, "but how can I help it when you will not weep for yourselves, although your immortal souls are on the verge of destruction, and for aught I know, you are

hearing your last sermon and may never more have another opportunity to have Christ offered to you?"[65]

I constantly find myself wishing that we preachers could learn to weep again. Many things seem to stop us from crying over the lost sinners on the broad road which leads to destruction. Some preachers are so caught up in the joyful celebration of salvation that they never think to weep over those who are rejecting it. Others have been deceived by the devil's lie of universalism: everybody will be saved in the end, they say, and nobody will be lost. Their eyes are dry because they have closed them to the awful reality of eternal death and outer darkness of which both Jesus and his apostles spoke. Others faithfully warn sinners of hell, but do so casually or with a sick pleasure. This is almost more terrible than the blindness of those who ignore or deny its reality.

A congregation learns the seriousness of the gospel by the seriousness with which their pastors preach it. "We must not talk to our congregations," said Spurgeon to his students, "as if we were half-asleep. Our preaching must not be articulate snoring."[66] One thing is certain: if we ourselves grow sleepy over our message, our listeners can hardly be expected to stay awake.

Mind and Heart

The New Testament makes it clear that combining the mind and the heart, the rational and the emotional, can bring our listeners to faith and obedience. Paul reasoned and argued with people, using the Scriptures through the power of the Holy Spirit to try to turn them to God. But he also wept over them – just as his Master had done.

Consider how he combines teaching and pleading in his letters. 2 Corinthians 5 contains one of the major explanations of the doctrine of reconciliation in the New Testament. Paul explains that "God was reconciling the world to himself in Christ", that God was "not counting people's sins against them" and that for our sake he actually made Christ who "had no sin to be sin for us, so that in him we might become the righteousness of God" (vv. 19–21). Here are tightly packed truths about God's actions, about Christ and his cross, about sin, reconciliation and righteousness, which commentators are still struggling to unpack and explain. Yet Paul is not content just to make a deep theological statement. He goes beyond the fact of reconciliation to the message of reconciliation, beyond what God did in Christ to what he now does in us. He is an ambassador for God, begging his readers to "be reconciled to God" (v. 20). He did not stop with the exposition, but went on to the appeal. But the appeal came only after he had conveyed the truth.

Some preachers have no fear of enthusiasm; they make endless appeals for decision or conversion. In fact, their sermons are sometimes nothing but one long appeal. Yet their listeners are bewildered, because they have not understood (or been helped to understand) the nature or basis of the appeal. To ask for a decision without doctrine is an offence to human beings, for it suggests a mindless manipulation.

Other preachers make the opposite mistake. They explain the central biblical doctrines precisely. They are faithful to the content of Scripture. They explain it clearly and apply the lessons to today's world. Yet somehow they appear cold and distant. There is no urgency in their voice, and no tear is ever seen in their eyes. They would never dream of leaning over the pulpit to beg sinners in the name of Christ to repent, to come to him and to be reconciled with God.

What is needed today is Paul's combination of reason and emotion, of teaching and pleading. J. W. Alexander begs for "theological preaching". What interests people, he says, is "argument made red-hot".[67] A twentieth-century British preacher who made a similar point was Dr. Campbell Morgan, minister of Westminster Chapel, London. The three essentials of a sermon, he told his students, are "truth, clarity and passion".[68] He told a tale of a preacher who asked a great actor how he could draw such crowds by fiction, while he was preaching the truth and not getting any crowd at all. "This is quite simple," replied the actor. "I present my fiction as though it were truth; you present your truth as though it were fiction."[69]

Dr. Martyn Lloyd-Jones also shared this conviction.

> Logic on fire! Eloquent reason! Are these contradictions? Of course they are not. Reason concerning this truth ought to be mightily eloquent, as you see it in the case of the Apostle Paul

and others. It is theology on fire. And a theology which does not take fire, I maintain, is a defective theology, or at least the man's understanding of it is defective. Preaching is theology coming through a man who is on fire.[70]

We need to remember that the Holy Spirit is both "the Spirit of truth" and the one who appeared on the Day of Pentecost in "tongues of fire". Since the two are not separated in him, they will not be separate in the Spirit-filled Christian either. Once we allow him his freedom, both in the preparation and delivery of our sermons, the light and the fire, the truth and the passion will be reunited.

We also need to remember the experience of the two disciples with whom Jesus walked to Emmaus on the first Easter afternoon. When he vanished, they said to one another, "Were not our hearts burning within us while he talked with us on the road and opened the Scriptures to us? (Luke 24:32). They were deeply moved. Fire had begun to burn within them when they glimpsed new truths. It is still truth – the Christ-centred, biblical truth – that sets the heart on fire.

Humour in the Pulpit

At first sight, seriousness and humour may seem to be contradictory. However, the issue is not so simple. Jesus used humour in his teaching, as for example, when he talked about people who "strain out a gnat but swallow a camel (Matt 23:24):

> How many of us have ever pictured the process, and the series of sensations, as the long hairy neck slid down the throat of the Pharisee – all that amplitude of loose-hung anatomy – the hump – two humps – both of them slid down – and he never noticed – and the legs – all of them – with the whole outfit of knees and big padded feet. The Pharisee swallowed a camel and never noticed it.[71]

But humour has to be used wisely at the right place and the right time. "The evident purpose of Christ's humour is to clarify and increase understanding, rather than to hurt. Perhaps some hurt is inevitable, especially when ... human pride is rendered ridiculous, but the clear aim is something other than harm ... Truth, and truth alone is the end."[72]

We must never joke about serious topics. But humour may be used to break tension, so that people can relax before concentrating again. It may be used to break down people's defences – to move them from stubbornness and rebellion to responsiveness. Finally, it can help us to laugh at ourselves and shame us into repentance. As James Aggrey, a founder of Achimota College in Ghana, said, "I get their mouths open in a laugh, and ram the truth down."[73] Or to put in another way, "after the mirthquake the still small voice".[74]

Conclusion

Sincerity and earnestness cannot be put on like decorations on Christmas trees. They are the fruit of the Spirit. They describe a person who believes and feels what he says. "The man, the whole man, lies behind the sermon. Preaching is not the performance of an hour. It is the outflow of a life. It takes twenty years to make a sermon, because it takes twenty years to make the man."[75]

James Black put it similarly, "the best preaching is always the natural overflow of a ripe mind and the expression of a growing experience. A good sermon is never worked up but worked out."[76] I like those two words "outflow" and "overflow". True preaching is never a superficial activity; it wells up out of the depths. Without the spring of the Holy Spirit's life within us, the rivers of living water can never flow from within us. It is out of the overflow of the heart that the mouth speaks (John 4:14; 7:37–39; Matt 12:34).

7

COURAGE AND HUMILITY

There is an urgent need for courageous preachers who, like the apostles will be "filled with the Holy Spirit" and will speak "the word of God boldly" (Acts 4:31, compare v. 13). People-pleasers and time-fillers never make good preachers. We are called to the holy task of biblical exposition and are appointed to proclaim what God has said, not what people want to hear.

Many in our churches "turn their ears away from the truth", and look for "teachers to say what their itching ears want to hear" (2 Tim 4:3, 4). But we should not scratch their itch or indulge them. We are to be like Paul who twice reminded the Ephesians that he had "not hesitated to preach anything that would be helpful" to them, proclaiming "the whole will of God" (Acts 20:20, 27). We have to beware of choosing texts and topics to suit our likes and dislikes or popular fashion. "People are driven from the church … not so much by stern truth that makes them uneasy as by weak nothings that make them contemptuous."[77] Yet many preachers get caught in the snare of fear (Prov 29:25). Once ensnared, we are no longer free; we have become the servants of public opinion.

The Tradition of Courageous Preaching

There have been many courageous preachers. Moses heard, believed, obeyed and taught the word of God, in spite of opposition and resulting loneliness. Elijah stood alone to fight for religious truth and social justice as he challenged the prophets of Baal and condemned the king and queen for murdering Naboth. Nathan dared to challenge King David about his adultery with Bathsheba and his murder of her husband. Amos spoke out against evil in the king's sanctuary at Bethel and foretold a horrible fate for Amaziah who tried to silence him. Jeremiah, although a patriot, was accused of hating his own country because he faithfully conveyed God's words.

This tradition of courage includes John the Baptist. John was neither a reed blown by public opinion nor an aristocrat satisfying his own desires; he was a true prophet, controlled by the word of God (Matt 11:7–11). His courage cost him his life. He was the last of the long line of prophets whom Israel rejected and killed (Matt 23:29–36; Acts 7:52) before killing their Messiah and opposing his apostles (1 Thess 2:15).

Jesus himself spoke fearlessly. Towards the end of his life the disciples of the Pharisees, admitted: "Teacher, we know that you are a man of integrity and that you teach the way of God in accordance with the truth. You aren't swayed by others, because you pay no attention to who they are" (Matt 22:16). It is not surprising that his popularity in Galilee lasted only about a year, nor that the authorities decided to kill him.

Jesus warned his followers that if the teacher was persecuted, his disciples would also be persecuted. And so it happened, a direct result of the boldness of their witness to Jesus. Peter and John were imprisoned. Stephen and James were martyred. Paul suffered greatly. From prison Paul wrote to ask his friends to pray that he might be given the words "so that I may fearlessly make [the gospel] known" (Eph 6:19, 20). Instead of silencing him, his imprisonment gave him new opportunities for courageous testimony. The book of Acts ends with him under house arrest in Rome, still welcoming all who visited him, and still preaching and teaching "with all boldness and without hindrance" (Acts 28:30, 31).

This tradition of courageous witness and consequent suffering has continued throughout church history. Chrysostom in the fourth century preached with great power and courage, first in Antioch and then for six years as Archbishop of Constantinople, until he offended the empress and was banished. He spoke out bravely against evil in the city, and "rebuked without fear or favour all classes and conditions of men".[78] John Wycliffe, the forerunner of the English Reformation, opposed the church leaders, criticizing their worldliness, the corruption of the pope and the error of transubstantiation. He was put on trial several times, but his friends defended him and he escaped condemnation. However, many of his followers were burned as heretics. Luther is on record as saying that "Whoever wants to do his duty as a preacher ... must denounce anyone that needs to be denounced – great or small, rich or poor or powerful, friend or foe".[79]

The Scottish reformer John Knox was physically weak, but he had a fiery nature and spoke forcefully. After his return to Scotland in 1559, his courageous preaching encouraged the Scots who longed for a reformed church. Summoned before the queen, whom he had offended with his preaching, he told her that in the pulpit "I am not master of myself, but must obey him who commands me to speak plain, and to flatter no flesh upon the face of the earth."[80]

In the twentieth century there were many courageous preachers worldwide who refused to edit their message to make it more popular. One was Archbishop Janani Luwum of Uganda, who was murdered in 1977 because of his denunciation of the excesses of Idi Amin. Another was Martin Luther King Senior, the father of the assassinated black American civil rights leader, who is described as "a big man, physically and spiritually. He stands strong and broad in his pulpit, afraid of no man, white or black, telling it like it is, preaching the word to his congregation and giving them his overflowing love."[81]

To Comfort and Disturb

Preachers, like prophets, believe they bring a word from God, and are not free to change it. Therefore all preachers have at various times to choose between truth with unpopularity and falsehood with popularity.

The gospel still offends, and nobody who preaches it faithfully can expect to escape all opposition. People today resent the exclusiveness of the Christian faith, and they resent the humiliation of being unable to reach God through their own wisdom or goodness. Christ from his cross seems to say, "I am here because of you. If it were not for your sin and pride, I would not be here. And if you could have saved yourself, I would not be here either." The Christian pilgrimage begins with bowed head and bent knee at the cross; there is no other way into the kingdom of God.

Towards the end of his ministry, Alexander Whyte came to a crisis on this very issue. He knew that some people felt he over-emphasized sin, and he was tempted to soften that aspect of his preaching. But one day while he was walking:

> What seemed to me to be a Divine Voice spoke with all-commanding power in my conscience, and said to me as clear as clear could be: "No! Go on, and flinch not! Go back and boldly finish the work that has been given you to do. Speak out and fear not. Make them at any cost to see themselves in God's holy law as in a glass. Do you that, for no one else will do it. No one else will so risk his life and his reputation as to do it. And you have not much of either left to risk. Go home and spend what is left of your life in your appointed task of showing my people their sin and their need of my salvation."

He did, with the "fresh authority and fresh encouragement" imparted by this heavenly vision.[82]

Preachers cannot escape this duty of disturbing their listeners. We know that Christ spoke many comforting words, some of which are repeated in many Communion services. But not all his words were comforting; some were deeply disturbing. We must be like him and preach about God's anger as well as his love, grace and mercy; judgment as well as salvation; hell as well as heaven; death without Christ as well as resurrection with him; repentance as well as faith; Christ as Lord as well as Saviour; the cost as well as the rewards of Christian discipleship; self-denial as the path to self discovery; and the yoke of Christ's authority under which we find our rest.

Are we faithful in teaching what the apostles taught about relationships between husbands and wives, parents and children, masters and servants? Do we point out that envy is idolatry, that wealth is dangerous, and that Christians are called to care for one another? Do we insist that lifelong heterosexual marriage is God's choice for sexual fulfilment; that divorce (even if it is sometimes allowed because of human sinfulness) is never God's ideal? Do we preach that heterosexual adultery and immorality as well as homosexual practices are contrary to his will? Do our listeners know that God created work to allow us to be partners with him, to serve others and to know self-fulfilment, and that unemployment is a tragedy?

Yet the more we feel it necessary, in these sinful days, to preach about the judgment of God, the more we also need to stress his mercy towards sinners. Jesus spoke out fiercely against the hypocrisy of the scribes and Pharisees, yet he was called the friend of sinners. Sinners flocked round him and listened to him gladly. He invited them to come to him with their burdens and promised to give them rest. He accepted the affection of a forgiven prostitute, and told the woman caught in adultery, "Neither do I condemn you. Go now and leave your life of sin" (John 8:11).

It is significant that Paul appealed to the Corinthians with "the meekness and gentleness of Christ" (2 Cor 10:1). Yet he expected the churches to discipline offenders and even to excommunicate those who did not repent. It is obvious that he found no pleasure in these things. Indeed, he compared himself to a mother taking care of her children and to a loving father (1 Thess 2:7, 11).

Every Christian pastor today should have the same feelings of tender love towards those who have been committed to his care. As we speak to them every Sunday, we know some of the burdens they are bearing. As we look at their faces, we know that almost everybody has been bruised by life. We know they are feeling the pressure of temptation, defeat, depression, loneliness or despair. While it is true that some need to be disturbed from their self-satisfaction, others need the comfort of God's love above all else.

We need to pray for sensitivity to find the right balance so that we can, "disturb the comfortable and comfort the disturbed".[83] Like John Newton, the converted slave-trader, we must aim "to break a hard heart and to heal a broken heart".[84]

The Value of Systematic Exposition

Because it takes courage to deal with certain issues I recommend systematic exposition, working steadily through a book of the Bible or a section of a book, verse by verse or paragraph by paragraph. This approach forces us to discuss passages that we might otherwise overlook, or even deliberately avoid.

I remember preaching through the Sermon on the Mount, and coming to Matthew 5:31, 32, in which our Lord deals with the subject of divorce. Although I had been in the pastoral ministry for twenty-five years, to my shame I had never preached on this topic despite the fact that it is major issue today. Of course I could have made a number of excuses. "It's a very complex subject, and I don't have the necessary expertise." "It's also controversial, and I don't want to stir up trouble." "I'd be sure to offend somebody." But now I was leading the congregation through the Sermon on the Mount, and I could not possibly skip verses 31 and 32. No, I had to do what I had so long neglected, spending hours in study and thought before doing so.

A second benefit of this approach to preaching is that people will not be curious about why we choose a particular text on a particular Sunday. If I had suddenly preached on divorce, church members would have wondered, "Who is he aiming at today?" But, because they knew these were the next verses in the chapter through which I was preaching, their attention was not distracted by such questions.

The third benefit is probably the greatest: it models how to read the Bible. This deep, organized opening-up of a large portion of Scripture broadens people's thinking, introduces them to some of the Bible's major themes, and shows them how to interpret Scripture by Scripture. P. T. Forsyth explains:

> We need to be defended from [the preacher's] subjectivity, his excursions, his monotony, his limitations. We need, moreover, to protect him from the peril of preaching himself or his age. We must all preach *to* our age, but woe to us if it is our age we preach, and only hold up the mirror to the time.[85]

He stresses that one of a preacher's tasks is to rescue the Bible from the approach that

> reduces it to a religious scrapbook, and uses it only in verses and phrases ... He must cultivate more the free, large and organic treatment of the Bible, where each part is most valuable for its contribution to a living, evangelical whole, and where that whole is articulated into the great course of human history.[86]

For the health of the church, which lives and grows through the word of God, and for the sake of the preacher who needs this discipline, we must return to systematic exposition. In doing so, however, we need to consider our audience carefully and not feed them more than they can cope with. Not all congregations are spiritually mature or hungry enough to digest long expositions over many months. But if we take a paragraph (or several paragraphs or even a chapter) and work through it for a few weeks or months, our hearers will be well fed, while learning how to study the Scriptures for themselves. And we preachers will grow the courage we need to unfold the whole wisdom of God.

Humility

Unfortunately, our decision to be courageous in the pulpit can result in our becoming stubborn and arrogant. We may speak out, but may spoil it by becoming proud of our outspokenness. Pride is a major problem for any preacher and has ruined many, making their ministry powerless.

In some it is obvious. They seem almost to be repeating the boastful words of Nebuchadnezzar, "Is not this the great Babylon I have built … by my mighty power and for the glory of my majesty?" (Dan 4:28–37) "Would to God," says Henry Ward Beecher, "that these preachers, like Nebuchadnezzar, might go to grass for a time if, like him, they would return sane and humble."[87]

In other preachers, however, pride is more indirect, more deceptive, and more troublesome. It is possible to seem humble while constantly longing for praise. At the very moment we are glorifying Christ, we can actually be looking for our own glory. When we are pleading with the congregation to praise God, or even leading them in praise, we can be secretly hoping that they will spare a bit of praise for us. We need to cry out with Baxter, "O what a constant companion, what a tyrannical commander, what a sly, subtle and insinuating enemy is this sin of pride!"[88]

We have to fight this enemy. One way to do so is to remind ourselves that above all humility is about "walking humbly with your God" (Mic 6:8). We need to remember our calling to submit to the word of God, exalt our Master, and depend on the Holy Spirit. We need to value others more than ourselves, and gladly serve them (Phil 2:3, 4; 1 Pet 5:5). To do this requires a humble mind, humble motives and humble dependence.

The humble mind is neither closed nor uncritical, but it recognizes its limitations. It echoes Psalm 131:1: "My heart is not proud, Lord, my eyes are not haughty; I do not concern myself with great matters or things too wonderful for me." It recognizes that God is all-knowing and that "such knowledge is too wonderful for me; too lofty for me to attain" (Ps 139:6). The humble mind knows that God is beyond our understanding, that his thoughts and ways are higher than ours – just as the heavens are higher than the earth (Isa 55:8, 9). It realizes that without his self-revelation, we could never know him. It understands that "the foolishness of God is wiser than human wisdom" (1 Cor 1:25). We are foolish to imagine we could ever know his mind by ourselves, let alone instruct him or offer him advice (Rom 11:33, 34). We are not free, therefore, to contradict his revelation or to criticize his plan of salvation or the cross at the centre of it. God says, "I will destroy the wisdom of the wise" and in his wisdom saves us through the "foolishness" of the gospel (1 Cor 1:18–25; see also 3:18–20). It is our responsibility, therefore, to do everything we can, in ourselves and others, to "demolish arguments and every pretension that sets itself up against the knowledge of God, and [to] take captive every thought to make it obedient to Christ" (2 Cor 10:5).

This submission to God's revelation in Christ influences our preaching. The preacher with a humble mind will refuse to manipulate the biblical text in order to make it more acceptable to our day and age. Any attempt to make *it* more acceptable is really about making *ourselves* more acceptable or popular.

Adding to God's word was the fault of the Pharisees, and subtracting from it was the fault of the Sadducees. Jesus criticized them both, insisting that the word of God must be allowed to stand by itself, without pluses or minuses, without enlargement or change, supreme and complete in its authority. Anyone who refuses to submit to God's word and "does not agree to the sound instruction of our Lord Jesus Christ and to godly teaching" is among those who are "conceited and understand nothing" (1 Tim 6:3, 4; Titus 1:9, 10). Christian preachers are to be neither inventors of new doctrines nor editors who delete old doctrines. Rather, they are to be stewards, faithfully handing out scriptural truths to God's household. Nothing more, nothing less, and nothing else.

To ensure this, we need to come to the Scriptures daily, and to sit humbly, like Mary, at Jesus' feet, listening to his word. We must come expectantly for, as Jesus plainly stated, God hides his secrets from the wise and learned, and reveals them instead to little children, to humble, open-hearted seekers for the truth (Matt 11:25).

Humility of mind is to be accompanied by *humble motives.* Why do we preach? What do we hope to accomplish? Too often our motives are selfish. We desire the praise and the congratulations of men. We stand at the door after services and feast on the remarks our congregation make. To be sure, genuine words of appreciation can do much to boost a discouraged preacher. But idle flattery is damaging to the preacher and displeasing to God. Congregations should, therefore, be encouraged to be careful in their expressions of encouragement.

The main purpose of preaching is to expound Scripture so faithfully and relevantly that Jesus Christ is seen to be able to meet every need. The true preacher is a witness; he is constantly testifying to Christ. But without humility he neither can nor wants to do so. James Denney was well aware of this, and so he had the following words framed in the vestry of his Scottish church: "No man can bear witness to Christ and to himself at the same time. No man can give the impression that he himself is clever and that Christ is mighty to save."[89]

In other words, preaching is meant to encourage a meeting between God and the people. Donald G. Miller puts it more strongly. "No man has really preached until the two-sided encounter between him and his congregation has given way to a three-sided encounter, where God himself becomes one of the living parties to it."[90] I agree. The most moving experience a preacher can ever have is when, in the middle of the sermon, a strange hush descends upon the congregation. The sleepers have woken up, the coughers have stopped coughing, and the fidgeters are sitting still. No eyes or minds are wandering. Everybody is listening, but not to the preacher. The preacher is forgotten, and the people are face to face with the living God, listening to his still, small voice.

A biblical image may make this clearer. The Old Testament explained the relationship between Yahweh and Israel as a marriage, and in the New Testament, Jesus called himself the Bridegroom (Mark 2:19, 20). John the Baptist's role was to be his forerunner, sent ahead of him, like the best man at a wedding who wants to do all he can to ensure that the wedding goes well and that nothing comes between the bride and the bridegroom. As John said, "The bride belongs to the bridegroom. The friend who attends the bridegroom waits and listens for him, and is full of joy when he hears the bridegroom's voice. That joy is mine, and it is now complete. He must become greater; I must become less" (John 3:28–30). The preacher's ministry is like that of John the Baptist, preparing Christ's way, rejoicing in his voice, leaving him with his bride, and constantly decreasing in order that Christ may increase.

The Apostle Paul clearly saw this as his ministry. "I promised you to one husband, to Christ," he wrote to the Corinthians, 'so that I might present you as a pure virgin to him." He even felt jealous on behalf of Christ, because the bride was showing signs of unfaithfulness (2 Cor 11:2, 3). "We are to be the friends of the Bridegroom," said J. H. Jowett, "winning men, not to ourselves but to him, match-making for the Lord, abundantly satisfied when we have brought the bride and the bridegroom together."[91]

Finally, we must exhibit *a humble dependence*. Every preacher desires to be effective. We hope the people will listen to our sermons, understand them and respond in faith and obedience. But on what do we rely to achieve this?

Many rely on themselves. They are strong and outgoing. They may also have a sharp mind. So they make an impression on everybody they meet, for they are born leaders. They naturally expect to use these gifts while they are in the pulpit. Are they right to do so? Yes and no. Certainly, they should recognize these gifts as coming from God. They should not pretend that they lack these gifts, nor try to suppress them, nor neglect to use them. But they should not imagine that even God-given talents can bring people to Christ without the addition of God-given blessing.

We need to remember both the pitiful spiritual condition of people without Christ and the frightening strength and skill of the powers of darkness opposing us. Jesus talked about human lostness in terms of physical disability. By ourselves we are blind to God's truth and deaf to his voice. Lame, we cannot walk in his ways. Mute, we can neither sing to him nor speak for him. We are even dead in our trespasses and sins. We are also the slaves of demonic forces. Of course, if we think this is exaggerated or false, then we shall see no need for supernatural power. But if people are really spiritually and morally blind, deaf, dumb, lame and even dead or imprisoned by Satan, then it is ridiculous to imagine that by ourselves and our merely human preaching we can reach or rescue them.

Only Jesus Christ through his Holy Spirit can open blind eyes and deaf ears, make the lame walk and the dumb speak. Only he can wake up the conscience, enlighten the mind, fire the heart, move the will, give life to the dead and rescue slaves from Satan. Therefore, our greatest need as preachers is to be "clothed with power from on high" (Luke 24:49). Like the apostles, we must preach the gospel "by the Holy Spirit sent from heaven" (1 Pet 1:12). Then the gospel will come to people "not simply with words but also with power, with the Holy Spirit and deep conviction" (1 Thess 1:5).

Why is this power missing in our preaching? I strongly suspect that the main reason is our pride. In order to be filled with the Spirit, we must first acknowledge our own emptiness. In order to be used by God, we must first humble ourselves under his mighty hand (1 Pet 5:6). In order to receive his power, we must first admit and delight in our own weakness.

This idea of "power through weakness" is repeated again and again in Paul's letters to the Corinthians. The Corinthians were proud people, boastful about their own gifts and achievements and about their leaders. Paul was horrified! They were giving him the respect that was due to Christ alone. "Was Paul crucified for you?" he cries out in dismay. "Were you baptized into the name of Paul?" (1 Cor 1:13). "So then, no more boasting about human leaders" he insists. "Let those who boast boast in the Lord" (1 Cor 3:21; 1:31).

Against this background Paul's "power through weakness" theme stands out clearly. There are three main passages in which it occurs.

> I came to you in weakness with great fear and trembling. My message and my preaching were not with wise and persuasive words, but with a demonstration of the Spirit's power, *so that* your faith might not rest on human wisdom, but on God's power. (1 Cor 2:3–5)

> But we have this treasure in earthen vessels, *so that* the surpassing greatness of the power will be of God and not from ourselves. (2 Cor 4:7, NASB)

> Therefore, in order to keep me from becoming conceited, I was given a thorn in my flesh, a messenger of Satan, to torment me. Three times I pleaded with the Lord to take it away from me. But he said to me, "My grace is sufficient for you, for my power is made perfect in weakness." Therefore, I will boast all the more gladly about my weaknesses, *so that* Christ's power may rest on me. That is why, for Christ' sake, I delight in weaknesses, in insults, in hardships, in persecutions, in difficulties. For when I am weak, then I am strong. (2 Cor 12:7–10)

Note the repeated use of the words *so that*. Let me repeat Paul's statements in my own words:

"I was with you in personal weakness. I therefore relied on the Holy Spirit's powerful demonstration of the truth of my message, *so that* your faith might rest in God's power alone."

"We have the treasure of the gospel in fragile clay pots (that's how weak and brittle our bodies are) *so that* it may be plainly seen that the tremendous power which keeps us going and which converted you comes from God and not from ourselves."

"Because Jesus told me that his power is made perfect in human weakness, therefore I will gladly boast about my weaknesses, *so that* Christ's power may rest upon me … For it's only when I'm weak that I'm strong."

We cannot ignore the significance of this repeated phrase, or the conclusion to which it points. Human weakness was deliberately allowed to continue because through it the divine power could operate and be displayed. Paul recognized that his thorn in the flesh (whether physical or psychological) was "a messenger of Satan". But the Lord Jesus Christ rejected Paul's pleadings that it might be removed. It was given to humble him. And it was allowed to remain *so that* in his weakness, Christ's power might rest on him and be made perfect in him.

All preachers are limited, sinful, weak and imperfect "earthenware vessels" or "jars of clay". The power belongs to Christ and is deployed through his Spirit. The words we speak in human weakness, the Holy

Spirit carries by his power to the mind, heart, conscience and will of the hearers.

A mind which submits to the written word of God, a desire for Christ to meet with his people, and a dependence on the power of the Holy Spirit – this is the humility we need. Our message must be God's word, not ours; our aim Christ's glory, not ours; and our confidence the Holy Spirit's power, not ours.

EPILOGUE

This book was originally published under the title *I Believe in Preaching*. That title expresses a strong personal conviction. I do believe in preaching. I believe that true, biblical preaching is the one thing that can restore health and energy to the church and lead its members into maturity in Christ.

Certainly there are objections to it, which we have tried to face. But there are even stronger theological arguments for it, which we have tried to express. Certainly, the task of preaching today is extremely difficult, as we seek to build bridges between the word and the world, between divine revelation and human experience. So God calls us anew to give more time to study and to preparation. He calls us anew to decide to preach with sincerity, earnestness, courage and humility.

The privilege is great, the responsibility heavy, the temptations many, and the standards high. How can we hope to respond adequately?

I would like to share with you a simple secret. I myself struggle to remember it, but whenever I am made aware of it, I find it extremely helpful. It begins with the negative point made in Psalm 139: wherever we go, we cannot escape from God. But the psalm continues with the positive message that, wherever we are, "even there" his right hand leads and holds us. Moreover, his "loving eye" is on us, and his ears are open to our words and prayers (Pss 32:8; 34:15; 1 Pet 3:12). This truth is important for every Christian, but it is especially important to the preacher, as Jeremiah and Paul confirm.

> Jeremiah: "What passes my lips is open before you." (Jer 17:16)

Paul: "In Christ we speak before God with sincerity, as those sent from God." (2 Cor 2:17)

"We have been speaking in the sight of God as those in Christ." (2 Cor 12:19)

True, we preach in the sight and the hearing of people, and they challenge us to be faithful. But much more challenging is the awareness that we preach in the sight and hearing of God. He sees what we do; he listens to what we say. To him all hearts are open and from him no secrets are hidden. Nothing will rid us of laziness and coldness, of hypocrisy, cowardice and pride more than the knowledge that God sees, hears and takes note.

May God grant us a more constant and clear awareness of his presence. God grant that when we preach, we may become even more conscious that he sees and hears, and that this knowledge will inspire us to faithfulness!

APPENDIX 1

THE GLORY OF PREACHING: A HISTORICAL SKETCH

The importance of preaching has been recognized throughout church history, as a quick historical survey will show.

Jesus and His Apostles

The writers of the Gospels repeatedly present Jesus as a preacher. He set out "to teach and preach in the towns of Galilee" (Matt 11:1) and Judea (Luke 4:44). In the synagogue at Nazareth, he announced that this was the task for which he had been sent, in fulfilment of the prophecy in Isaiah 61 (Luke 4:16–20, 43; see also Mark 1:38). He accepted the title of "Rabbi" or "Teacher" (John 4:31; 9:2). When questioned by the High Priest, he said that he had "spoken openly to the world" and had "said nothing in secret" (John 18:20). He told Pilate that he had come "to testify to the truth" (John 18:37).

Jesus also sent his disciples out to preach, initially to "the lost sheep of Israel" (Matt 10:6), and later to "all nations" (Matt 28:19; Luke 24:47). The disciples obeyed him: "Then the disciples went out and preached everywhere" (Mark 16:20). The apostles did not allow themselves to be distracted by other tasks but gave their attention to "prayer and the ministry of the word" (Acts 6:4). This was the task to which Jesus had called them.

In Acts we are told that Peter and the others in Jerusalem "spoke the word of God boldly" (Acts 4:31). We see Paul undertaking three missionary journeys because he felt compelled to preach (1 Cor 9:16).

Even under house arrest, he "proclaimed the kingdom of God and taught about the Lord Jesus Christ – with all boldness and without hindrance" (Acts 28:31). He knew that preaching was God's appointed way for sinners to hear about the Saviour, and that without preaching the message would not be heard (Rom 10:14). At the end of his life Paul passed his commission on to young Timothy, instructing him to "preach the word, be prepared in season and out of season; correct, rebuke and encourage – with great patience and careful instruction" (2 Tim 4:1, 2).

The Church Fathers

We find the same emphasis on preaching among the early church fathers. The *Didache,* a church manual dating from early in the second century, mentions various teaching ministries. It states that travelling teachers are to be welcomed provided they are genuine. (False teachers could be identified by the fact that their teaching would contradict the apostolic faith and by their conduct – they would stay for more than two days, ask for money and fail to practice what they preached).[92] Genuine teachers should be listened to with humility, "always trembling at the words which you have heard". Believers should "remember night and day him who speaks the word of God to you, and honour him as you do the Lord".[93]

In about the middle of the second century, Justin Martyr published a document known as his *First Apology* in which he argued that Christianity is true because Christ is the embodiment of truth and the Saviour of all. Towards the end of this document, he described the worship of the Christians of his day, which emphasized the reading and preaching of the Scriptures:

> And on the day called Sunday, all who live in cities or in the country gather together to one place, and the memoirs of the apostles or the writings of the prophets are read, as long as time permits; then, when the reader has ceased, the president verbally instructs, and exhorts, to the imitation of these good things.[94]

The Latin father Tertullian also published an *Apology* at the end of the second century. In it he emphasized the love and unity between Christians and described their meetings:

> We assemble to read our sacred writings ... With the sacred words
> we nourish our faith, we animate our hope, we make our confidence
> more steadfast, and no less by inculcations of God's precepts we
> confirm good habits. In the same place also exhortations are
> made, rebukes and sacred censures are administered.[95]

One of the most famous of the early Christian preachers is John Chrysostom,
who became Bishop of Constantinople in A.D. 398. He was given the
nickname *Chrysostomos* or "golden-mouthed" and is still "regarded as the
greatest pulpit orator of the Greek church" and "a model for preachers
in large cities".[96] In a sermon based on Ephesians 6:13, Chrysostom
pointed out that, like our human body, the body of Christ is subject to
many diseases. While there are many things we can do to restore our own
physical health, what can be done to heal Christ's body when it is diseased?

> One only means and one way of cure has been given us ... and
> that is teaching of the word. This is the best instrument, this
> the best diet and climate; this serves instead of medicine, this
> serves instead of cautery and cutting; whether it be needful
> to burn or to amputate, this one method must be used; and
> without it nothing else will avail.[97]

Chrysostom's preaching was memorable for a number of reasons. First, he
was biblical. Not only did he preach systematically through several books,
but his sermons were full of biblical quotations and allusions. Secondly,
his interpretation of Scripture was simple and straightforward. Thirdly,
his moral applications were down-to-earth. Reading them, we get a vivid
picture of the life of the city in which he lived – the pomp of the imperial
court, the luxuries of the aristocracy, the wild races at the hippodrome.
Fourthly, he was fearless in his condemnation of wrongdoing. Because of
his faithful preaching he was driven into exile, where he died.

The Friars and the Reformers

Moving rapidly on to the start of the second millennium, we see the rise
of Roman Catholic orders that celebrated preaching. The founder of
the Franciscan order, Francis of Assisi (1182–1226), was as committed

to preaching as he was to a life of service and poverty. He insisted that "unless you preach everywhere you go, there is no use to go anywhere to preach."[98] His contemporary Dominic (1170–1221) travelled widely in the cause of the gospel and organized his followers into an Order of Preachers that became known as the Dominican Friars. Prominent leaders of these orders even went so far as to assert that listening to preaching was even more important than attending mass.[99]

Given this focus on preaching the word of God, it is not surprising to see the rise of the forerunner or "morning star" of the Reformation, Oxford's John Wycliffe (1329–1384). He gradually came to see that the Holy Scripture must be the supreme authority in faith and life and spearheaded the first full translation of the Latin Bible into English. Himself a diligent biblical preacher, Wycliffe had no doubt about the chief task of the clergy:

> The highest service that man may attain to on earth is to preach the word of God. … And for this cause, Jesus Christ left other works and occupied himself mostly in preaching, and thus did his apostles, and for this, God loved them. … The church … is honoured most by the preaching of God's word, and hence this is the best service that priests may render unto God.[100]

During the Renaissance, men like Erasmus and Thomas More studied the Bible and the writings of the early church leaders. As a result, they began to criticize the corruption in the church and to call for reform based on the word of God. Recognizing that preachers must play a key role in this, Erasmus wrote:

> The most important function of the priest is teaching, by which he may instruct, admonish, chide and console. A layman can baptize. All the people can pray. The priest does not always baptize, he does not always absolve, but he should always teach. What good is it to be baptized if one has not been catechized; what good to go to the Lord's Table if one does not know what it means?[101]

These words explain the old saying that "Erasmus laid the egg that Luther hatched", for Martin Luther (1483–1546) agreed with and expanded on Erasmus' emphasis on teaching. Like other leaders of the

Reformation, he regarded the pulpit as more important than the altar. People would be saved by hearing and accepting God's word, not by simply attending mass and receiving the elements.

Luther stressed the liberating power of the word of God and its importance for our spiritual life: "The church owes its life to the word of promise, and is nourished and preserved by this same word."[102] He insisted that

> the soul can do without all things except the word of God ... if it has the word it is rich and lacks nothing, since this word is the word of life, of truth, of light, of peace, of righteousness, of salvation, of joy, of liberty. ... To preach Christ means to feed the soul, to make it righteous, to set it free and to save it.[103]

Given this high view of the word of God, it is not surprising that Luther regarded preaching as the "highest and only duty and obligation" of every bishop and pastor.[104] He identified nine characteristics of a good preacher. He should "teach systematically ... have a ready wit [intellect], ... be eloquent, ... have a good voice and ... a good memory". He should also "know when to make an end ... [and] ... be sure of his doctrine". He said that the ultimate test of a good preacher is whether he is prepared to face ridicule and to lose his life, his wealth and his good name because of his preaching.[105]

Luther lived by these high demands. Enduring both religious and political persecution, he insisted that "even if I were to lose my body and my life on account of it, I cannot depart from the true word of God".[106]

John Calvin (1509–1564), too, was committed to preaching the word of God to ordinary Christians of all ages, including those who were unable to read it for themselves. He expounded Scripture verse by verse and chapter by chapter, paying close attention to both the historical and the theological context. He also published his *Institutes of the Christian Religion* and many commentaries to help pastors become better preachers.

Calvin's message was taken up by the English Reformers when formulating Article 19 of the Thirty-Nine Articles of the Anglican Church: "The visible church of Christ is a congregation of faithful [believing] men in which the pure word of God is preached, and the sacraments be duly ministered according to Christ's ordinance." The Anglican ordination service required the bishop to give each ordinand a Bible as a symbol of his office and to urge him to be "studious ... in reading and learning the Scriptures", authorizing him by the power of the Holy Spirit "to preach the word of God and to minister the holy sacraments in the congregation".

The Puritans and the Evangelicals

The seventeenth-century Puritans have been called many things, not all of them complimentary. But the name which best sums them up is "godly preachers". Like the Reformers, they gave great prominence to preaching. One of them, Richard Baxter (1615–1691), was so disturbed by the ignorance, laziness and licentiousness of the clergy that he wrote a book called *The Reformed Pastor* (published in 1656 and still in print!). He shared the principles which directed his own pastoral work:

> We must teach them, as much as we can, of the word and works of God. Oh what two volumes are these for a minister to preach upon! How great, how excellent, how wonderful and mysterious! All Christians are disciples or scholars of Christ; the church is his school, we are his ushers [assistant teachers]; the Bible is his grammar [textbook]; this is it that we must be daily teaching them.[107]

Baxter's teaching took two forms. On the one hand, he and his assistant personally instructed each family in the parish at least once a year. Each family was invited to visit him for about an hour. During these visits family members would be asked to recite the catechism, be helped to understand it, and be questioned about their personal experience of its truths. These visits took up two whole days each week. The other aspect of his work was the public preaching of the word, a work that he insisted,

> requireth greater skill and especially greater life and zeal, than any of us bring to it. It is no small matter to stand up in the face of a congregation and deliver a message as from the living God, in the name of our Redeemer. [108]

A few years later, Cotton Mather of Boston (1663–1728) provided "Directions for a Candidate of the Ministry" in his book, *Student and Preacher*. His preface begins:

> The office of the Christian ministry, rightly understood, is the most honourable, and important, that any man in the whole world can ever sustain; and it will be one of the wonders and employments of eternity to consider the reasons why the wisdom and goodness of God assigned this office to imperfect and guilty man! ... The great design and intention of the office of a Christian preacher are to restore the throne and dominion of God in the souls of men; to display in the most lively colours, and proclaim in the clearest language, the wonderful perfections, offices and grace of the Son of God; and to attract the souls of men into a state of everlasting friendship with him.[109]

In 1738 a young man named John Wesley attended a meeting in Aldersgate Street in London, where his heart was warmed as he put his "trust in Christ, in Christ only for salvation". Assured that his sins had been taken away and that Christ had saved him from the law of sin and death, he at once began to preach the free salvation he had received. Influenced by his reading of Baxter, he encouraged house-to-house ministry and catechizing of converts. But above all he was a preacher, who addressed vast crowds in churches and churchyards, on village greens, in fields and natural amphitheatres. "I do indeed live by preaching" he wrote in his journal. His textbook was always the Bible, for he knew that its overriding purpose was to point to Christ and to show the way to salvation:

> O give me that book! At any price, give me the book of God! I have it: here is knowledge enough for me. Let me be *homo unius libri* [a man of one book]. Here then I am, far from the busy ways of men. I sit down alone: only God is here. In his presence I open, I read his book; for this end, to find the way to heaven.[110]

John Wesley preached what he learned from these biblical meditations, sharing with others what he had found, and pointing the way to heaven and holiness.

Although John Wesley has become better known, his younger contemporary George Whitefield (1714–1770) was almost certainly the more powerful preacher. In Britain and America, indoors and out of doors, he averaged about twenty sermons a week for thirty-four years! Eloquent, zealous, dogmatic, passionate, he enlivened his preaching with vivid metaphors, down-to-earth illustrations and dramatic gestures. He held audiences spellbound as he addressed direct questions to them or begged them earnestly to be reconciled with God. He had complete confidence in the authority of his message, and was determined that it should receive the respect it deserved as God's word. Once when he was preaching he "noticed an old man settling down for his accustomed, sermon-time nap". Whitefield began his sermon quietly, without disturbing him. But then he said,

> "If I had come to speak to you in my own name, you might go to sleep! … But I have come to you in the name of the Lord God of hosts, and (he clapped his hands and stamped his foot) I *must* and I *will* be heard." The old man woke up startled.[111]

The Nineteenth Century

Charles Simeon (1759–1836) was converted while an undergraduate at Cambridge University and longed to preach the gospel there. Walking past Holy Trinity Church in the heart of the campus, he used to say to himself, "How should I rejoice if God were to give me that church, that I might preach his gospel there, and be a herald for him in the midst of the university."[112] God answered his prayer, and in 1782 he became pastor there. At first, however, he met violent opposition, but he persevered and over the years he won the respect of all. For fifty-four years he systematically opened up the Scriptures there, determined "to know nothing except Jesus Christ and him crucified" as his memorial stone tells us. Simeon declared that

> ministers are ambassadors for God, and speak in Christ's stead. If they preach what is founded on the Scriptures, their word, as far as it is agreeable to the mind of God, is to be considered

as God's. This is asserted by our Lord and his apostles. We ought therefore to receive the preacher's word as the word of God himself.[113]

Throughout the nineteenth century, in spite of the emergence of higher criticism and the evolutionary theories of Charles Darwin, the pulpit maintained its prestige in England and America. People flocked to hear the great preachers of the day like John Henry Newman and Charles Haddon Spurgeon and eagerly read their printed sermons. We see something of this respect in Herman Melville's account of a sermon in *Moby Dick* (1851). The preacher stands in a pulpit shaped like the prow of a ship, which Melville considered appropriate for "the pulpit leads the world".[114] Few would make that claim today, but it would not have sounded like an exaggeration to Melville's readers.

The Twentieth Century

The twentieth century began in a mood of optimism. The West looked forward to stability, scientific progress and wealth; the church and preachers were respected. But, within a few years this optimism was shattered by the horrors of the First World War and the ensuing economic depression.

Yet confidence in the privilege and power of pulpit ministry survived. Theologians like Karl Barth, who had gained a new realism about humanity and a new faith in God, were convinced that preaching was even more important than before. In the days before World War II, preachers like Dietrich Bonhoeffer and Martin Niemöller showed great courage in preaching and equipping preachers, despite Hitler's rise to power. In this context of persecution, Bonhoeffer stressed the importance of preaching. So did the Swiss preacher Walter Lüthi, who became convinced, in the words of the Second Helvetic Confession, that "the preaching of the word of God is the word of God", and "set himself to the task of working through one book of the Bible after another and trying to find what those sacred oracles meant to his time and place".[115] In an essay on preaching, Lüthi writes that the act of preaching "is one of those things for which no one actually has true ability. The very moment a man thinks he has this ability, his preaching becomes art and grace draws back in grief."[116]

Although the Second World War accelerated the process of secularization in Europe, it did not quench preaching. The great Scottish academic and preacher James S. Stewart (1896–1990) could still write in his preface to his book, *Heralds of God,*

> I have chosen the title of this book to stress one fundamental fact, namely, that preaching exists not for the propagating of views, opinions or ideals, but for the proclamation of the mighty acts of God. This is demonstrably the New Testament conception of the preacher's task: and it is this that will always give preaching a basic and essential place at the very heart of Christian worship.[117]

Stewart was faithful to this vision. One of his students later wrote,

> He was an intensely biblical preacher. Stewart had a way of explaining a passage of Scripture that made it sound so simple. I never had the feeling that he was an ingenious interpreter of Scripture or had stupendous virtuosity. Once he got through the text, it was always so obvious … The man was simply a good man, and what he said I had to take as the word of God."[118]

In the second half of the century, the tide of preaching ebbed. Yet there were still voices in many churches calling for its renewal. The "Decree on The Ministry and Life of Priests" issued by the Second Vatican Council summoned Roman Catholic clergy to preach the gospel:

> Priests have as their primary duty the proclamation of the Gospel of God to all. … [They must] summon all men urgently to conversion and to holiness … Preaching must not present God's word in a general and abstract fashion only, but it must apply the perennial truth of the gospel to the concrete circumstances of life.[119]

Donald Coggan, Archbishop of Canterbury from 1974–1980, and himself an able preacher founded a College of Preachers in England. And many in the Reformed tradition were inspired by Martyn Lloyd-Jones, who ministered at Westminster Chapel in London from 1938–1968.

His medical training and early practice as a physician, his unshakeable commitment to the authority of Scripture and to the Christ of Scripture, his keen analytical mind, his penetrating insight into the human heart, and his passionate Welsh fire combined to make him the most powerful British preacher of the fifties and sixties. In *Preaching and Preachers* (1971) he declares,

> To me the work of preaching is the highest and the greatest and the most glorious calling to which anyone can ever be called ... the most urgent need in the Christian church today is true preaching. ... There is nothing like it. It is the greatest work in the world, the most thrilling, the most exciting, the most rewarding, and the most wonderful.[120]

This brief historical sketch is far from complete because it is limited to those whose views on preaching are recorded in Western books. Yet they were by no means the only good preachers, for God has raised up faithful teachers and preachers in many regions. Yet what this chapter does demonstrate is the length and breadth of the Christian tradition that accords great importance to preaching. Yes, there have been those who have disagreed, but they are the exceptions. The Christian consensus down the centuries has been that preaching is of vital importance. We should not lightly set aside this testimony.

APPENDIX 2

McCHEYNE'S
BIBLE READING PLAN

January 1	Genesis 1	Matthew 1	Ezra 1	Acts 1
January 2	Genesis 2	Matthew 2	Ezra 2	Acts 2
January 3	Genesis 3	Matthew 3	Ezra 3	Acts 3
January 4	Genesis 4	Matthew 4	Ezra 4	Acts 4
January 5	Genesis 5	Matthew 5	Ezra 5	Acts 5
January 6	Genesis 6	Matthew 6	Ezra 6	Acts 6
January 7	Genesis 7	Matthew 7	Ezra 7	Acts 7
January 8	Genesis 8	Matthew 8	Ezra 8	Acts 8
January 9	Genesis 9-10	Matthew 9	Ezra 9	Acts 9
January 10	Genesis 11	Matthew 10	Ezra 10	Acts 10
January 11	Genesis 12	Matthew 11	Nehemiah 1	Acts 11
January 12	Genesis 13	Matthew 12	Nehemiah 2	Acts 12
January 13	Genesis 14	Matthew 13	Nehemiah 3	Acts 13
January 14	Genesis 15	Matthew 14	Nehemiah 4	Acts 14
January 15	Genesis 16	Matthew 15	Nehemiah 5	Acts 15
January 16	Genesis 17	Matthew 16	Nehemiah 6	Acts 16
January 17	Genesis 18	Matthew 17	Nehemiah 7	Acts 17
January 18	Genesis 19	Matthew 18	Nehemiah 8	Acts 18
January 19	Genesis 20	Matthew 19	Nehemiah 9	Acts 19
January 20	Genesis 21	Matthew 20	Nehemiah 10	Acts 20
January 21	Genesis 22	Matthew 21	Nehemiah 11	Acts 21
January 22	Genesis 23	Matthew 22	Nehemiah 12	Acts 22
January 23	Genesis 24	Matthew 23	Nehemiah 13	Acts 23

January 24	Genesis 25	Matthew 24	Esther 1	Acts 24
January 25	Genesis 26	Matthew 25	Esther 2	Acts 25
January 26	Genesis 27	Matthew 26	Esther 3	Acts 26
January 27	Genesis 28	Matthew 27	Esther 4	Acts 27
January 28	Genesis 29	Matthew 28	Esther 5	Acts 28
January 29	Genesis 30	Mark 1	Esther 6	Romans 1
January 30	Genesis 31	Mark 2	Esther 7	Romans 2
January 31	Genesis 32	Mark 3	Esther 8	Romans 3
February 1	Genesis 33	Mark 4	Esther 9-10	Romans 4
February 2	Genesis 34	Mark 5	Job 1	Romans 5
February 3	Genesis 35-36	Mark 6	Job 2	Romans 6
February 4	Genesis 37	Mark 7	Job 3	Romans 7
February 5	Genesis 38	Mark 8	Job 4	Romans 8
February 6	Genesis 39	Mark 9	Job 5	Romans 9
February 7	Genesis 40	Mark 10	Job 6	Romans 10
February 8	Genesis 41	Mark 11	Job 7	Romans 11
February 9	Genesis 42	Mark 12	Job 8	Romans 12
February 10	Genesis 43	Mark 13	Job 9	Romans 13
February 11	Genesis 44	Mark 14	Job 10	Romans 14
February 12	Genesis 45	Mark 15	Job 11	Romans 15
February 13	Genesis 46	Mark 16	Job 12	Romans 16
February 14	Genesis 47	Luke 1:1-38	Job 13	1 Corinthians 1
February 15	Genesis 48	Luke 1:39-80	Job 14	1 Corinthians 2
February 16	Genesis 49	Luke 2	Job 15	1 Corinthians 3
February 17	Genesis 50	Luke 3	Job 16-17	1 Corinthians 4
February 18	Exodus 1	Luke 4	Job 18	1 Corinthians 5
February 19	Exodus 2	Luke 5	Job 19	1 Corinthians 6
February 20	Exodus 3	Luke 6	Job 20	1 Corinthians 7
February 21	Exodus 4	Luke 7	Job 21	1 Corinthians 8
February 22	Exodus 5	Luke 8	Job 22	1 Corinthians 9
February 23	Exodus 6	Luke 9	Job 23	1 Corinthians 10
February 24	Exodus 7	Luke 10	Job 24	1 Corinthians 11
February 25	Exodus 8	Luke 11	Job 25-26	1 Corinthians 12
February 26	Exodus 9	Luke 12	Job 27	1 Corinthians 13
February 27	Exodus 10	Luke 13	Job 28	1 Corinthians 14
February 28	Exodus 11:1-12:20	Luke 14	Job 29	1 Corinthians 15
March 1	Exodus 12:21-50	Luke 15	Job 30	1 Corinthians 16

March 2	Exodus 13	Luke 16	Job 31	2 Corinthians 1
March 3	Exodus 14	Luke 17	Job 32	2 Corinthians 2
March 4	Exodus 15	Luke 18	Job 33	2 Corinthians 3
March 5	Exodus 16	Luke 19	Job 34	2 Corinthians 4
March 6	Exodus 17	Luke 20	Job 35	2 Corinthians 5
March 7	Exodus 18	Luke 21	Job 36	2 Corinthians 6
March 8	Exodus 19	Luke 22	Job 37	2 Corinthians 7
March 9	Exodus 20	Luke 23	Job 38	2 Corinthians 8
March 10	Exodus 21	Luke 24	Job 39	2 Corinthians 9
March 11	Exodus 22	John 1	Job 40	2 Corinthians 10
March 12	Exodus 23	John 2	Job 41	2 Corinthians 11
March 13	Exodus 24	John 3	Job 42	2 Corinthians 12
March 14	Exodus 25	John 4	Proverbs 1	2 Corinthians 13
March 15	Exodus 26	John 5	Proverbs 2	Galatians 1
March 16	Exodus 27	John 6	Proverbs 3	Galatians 2
March 17	Exodus 28	John 7	Proverbs 4	Galatians 3
March 18	Exodus 29	John 8	Proverbs 5	Galatians 4
March 19	Exodus 30	John 9	Proverbs 6	Galatians 5
March 20	Exodus 31	John 10	Proverbs 7	Galatians 6
March 21	Exodus 32	John 11	Proverbs 8	Ephesians 1
March 22	Exodus 33	John 12	Proverbs 9	Ephesians 2
March 23	Exodus 34	John 13	Proverbs 10	Ephesians 3
March 24	Exodus 35	John 14	Proverbs 11	Ephesians 4
March 25	Exodus 36	John 15	Proverbs 12	Ephesians 5
March 26	Exodus 37	John 16	Proverbs 13	Ephesians 6
March 27	Exodus 38	John 17	Proverbs 14	Philippians 1
March 28	Exodus 39	John 18	Proverbs 15	Philippians 2
March 29	Exodus 40	John 19	Proverbs 16	Philippians 3
March 30	Leviticus 1	John 20	Proverbs 17	Philippians 4
March 31	Leviticus 2-3	John 21	Proverbs 18	Colossians 1
April 1	Leviticus 4	Psalms 1-2	Proverbs 19	Colossians 2
April 2	Leviticus 5	Psalms 3-4	Proverbs 20	Colossians 3
April 3	Leviticus 6	Psalms 5-6	Proverbs 21	Colossians 4
April 4	Leviticus 7	Psalms 7-8	Proverbs 22	1 Thessalonians 1
April 5	Leviticus 8	Psalms 9	Proverbs 23	1 Thessalonians 2
April 6	Leviticus 9	Psalms 10	Proverbs 24	1 Thessalonians 3
April 7	Leviticus 10	Psalms 11-12	Proverbs 25	1 Thessalonians 4

April 8	Leviticus 11-12	Psalms 13-14	Proverbs 26	1 Thessalonians 5
April 9	Leviticus 13	Psalms 15-16	Proverbs 27	2 Thessalonians 1
April 10	Leviticus 14	Psalms 17	Proverbs 28	2 Thessalonians 2
April 11	Leviticus 15	Psalms 18	Proverbs 29	2 Thessalonians 3
April 12	Leviticus 16	Psalms 19	Proverbs 30	1 Timothy 1
April 13	Leviticus 17	Psalms 20-21	Proverbs 31	1 Timothy 2
April 14	Leviticus 18	Psalms 22	Ecclesiastes 1	1 Timothy 3
April 15	Leviticus 19	Psalms 23-24	Ecclesiastes 2	1 Timothy 4
April 16	Leviticus 20	Psalms 25	Ecclesiastes 3	1 Timothy 5
April 17	Leviticus 21	Psalms 26-27	Ecclesiastes 4	1 Timothy 6
April 18	Leviticus 22	Psalms 28-29	Ecclesiastes 5	2 Timothy 1
April 19	Leviticus 23	Psalms 30	Ecclesiastes 6	2 Timothy 2
April 20	Leviticus 24	Psalms 31	Ecclesiastes 7	2 Timothy 3
April 21	Leviticus 25	Psalms 32	Ecclesiastes 8	2 Timothy 4
April 22	Leviticus 26	Psalms 33	Ecclesiastes 9	Titus 1
April 23	Leviticus 27	Psalms 34	Ecclesiastes 10	Titus 2
April 24	Numbers 1	Psalms 35	Ecclesiastes 11	Titus 3
April 25	Numbers 2	Psalms 36	Ecclesiastes 12	Philemon
April 26	Numbers 3	Psalms 37	Song of Solomon 1	Hebrews 1
April 27	Numbers 4	Psalms 38	Song of Solomon 2	Hebrews 2
April 28	Numbers 5	Psalms 39	Song of Solomon 3	Hebrews 3
April 29	Numbers 6	Psalms 40-41	Song of Solomon 4	Hebrews 4
April 30	Numbers 7	Psalms 42-43	Song of Solomon 5	Hebrews 5
May 1	Numbers 8	Psalms 44	Song of Solomon 6	Hebrews 6
May 2	Numbers 9	Psalms 45	Song of Solomon 7	Hebrews 7
May 3	Numbers 10	Psalms 46-47	Song of Solomon 8	Hebrews 8
May 4	Numbers 11	Psalms 48	Isaiah 1	Hebrews 9
May 5	Numbers 12-13	Psalms 49	Isaiah 2	Hebrews 10
May 6	Numbers 14	Psalms 50	Isaiah 3-4	Hebrews 11
May 7	Numbers 15	Psalms 51	Isaiah 5	Hebrews 12
May 8	Numbers 16	Psalms 52-54	Isaiah 6	Hebrews 13
May 9	Numbers 17-18	Psalms 55	Isaiah 7	James 1
May 10	Numbers 19	Psalms 56-57	Isaiah 8:1-9:7	James 2
May 11	Numbers 20	Psalms 58-59	Isaiah 9:8-10:4	James 3
May 12	Numbers 21	Psalms 60-61	Isaiah 10:5-34	James 4
May 13	Numbers 22	Psalms 62-63	Isaiah 11-12	James 5
May 14	Numbers 23	Psalms 64-65	Isaiah 13	1 Peter 1

May 15	Numbers 24	Psalms 66-67	Isaiah 14	1 Peter 2
May 16	Numbers 25	Psalms 68	Isaiah 15	1 Peter 3
May 17	Numbers 26	Psalms 69	Isaiah 16	1 Peter 4
May 18	Numbers 27	Psalms 70-71	Isaiah 17-18	1 Peter 5
May 19	Numbers 28	Psalms 72	Isaiah 19-20	2 Peter 1
May 20	Numbers 29	Psalms 73	Isaiah 21	2 Peter 2
May 21	Numbers 30	Psalms 74	Isaiah 22	2 Peter 3
May 22	Numbers 31	Psalms 75-76	Isaiah 23	1 John 1
May 23	Numbers 32	Psalms 77	Isaiah 24	1 John 2
May 24	Numbers 33	Psalms 78:1-39	Isaiah 25	1 John 3
May 25	Numbers 34	Psalms 78:40-72	Isaiah 26	1 John 4
May 26	Numbers 35	Psalms 79	Isaiah 27	1 John 5
May 27	Numbers 36	Psalms 80	Isaiah 28	2 John
May 28	Deuteronomy 1	Psalms 81-82	Isaiah 29	3 John
May 29	Deuteronomy 2	Psalms 83-84	Isaiah 30	Jude
May 30	Deuteronomy 3	Psalms 85	Isaiah 31	Revelation 1
May 31	Deuteronomy 4	Psalms 86-87	Isaiah 32	Revelation 2
June 1	Deuteronomy 5	Psalms 88	Isaiah 33	Revelation 3
June 2	Deuteronomy 6	Psalms 89	Isaiah 34	Revelation 4
June 3	Deuteronomy 7	Psalms 90	Isaiah 35	Revelation 5
June 4	Deuteronomy 8	Psalms 91	Isaiah 36	Revelation 6
June 5	Deuteronomy 9	Psalms 92-93	Isaiah 37	Revelation 7
June 6	Deuteronomy 10	Psalms 94	Isaiah 38	Revelation 8
June 7	Deuteronomy 11	Psalms 95-96	Isaiah 39	Revelation 9
June 8	Deuteronomy 12	Psalms 97-98	Isaiah 40	Revelation 10
June 9	Deuteronomy 13-14	Psalms 99-101	Isaiah 41	Revelation 11
June 10	Deuteronomy 15	Psalms 102	Isaiah 42	Revelation 12
June 11	Deuteronomy 16	Psalms 103	Isaiah 43	Revelation 13
June 12	Deuteronomy 17	Psalms 104	Isaiah 44	Revelation 14
June 13	Deuteronomy 18	Psalms 105	Isaiah 45	Revelation 15
June 14	Deuteronomy 19	Psalms 106	Isaiah 46	Revelation 16
June 15	Deuteronomy 20	Psalms 107	Isaiah 47	Revelation 17
June 16	Deuteronomy 21	Psalms 108-109	Isaiah 48	Revelation 18
June 17	Deuteronomy 22	Psalms 110-111	Isaiah 49	Revelation 19
June 18	Deuteronomy 23	Psalms 112-113	Isaiah 50	Revelation 20
June 19	Deuteronomy 24	Psalms 114-115	Isaiah 51	Revelation 21

June 20	Deuteronomy 25	Psalms 116	Isaiah 52	Revelation 22
June 21	Deuteronomy 26	Psalms 117-118	Isaiah 53	Matthew 1
June 22	Deuteronomy 27:1-28:19	Psalms 119:1-24	Isaiah 54	Matthew 2
June 23	Deuteronomy 28:20-68	Psalms 119:25-48	Isaiah 55	Matthew 3
June 24	Deuteronomy 29	Psalms 119:49-72	Isaiah 56	Matthew 4
June 25	Deuteronomy 30	Psalms 119:73-96	Isaiah 57	Matthew 5
June 26	Deuteronomy 31	Psalms 119:97-120	Isaiah 58	Matthew 6
June 27	Deuteronomy 32	Psalms 119:121-144	Isaiah 59	Matthew 7
June 28	Deuteronomy 33-34	Psalms 119:145-176	Isaiah 60	Matthew 8
June 29	Joshua 1	Psalms 120-122	Isaiah 61	Matthew 9
June 30	Joshua 2	Psalms 123-125	Isaiah 62	Matthew 10
July 1	Joshua 3	Psalms 126-128	Isaiah 63	Matthew 11
July 2	Joshua 4	Psalms 129-131	Isaiah 64	Matthew 12
July 3	Joshua 5	Psalms 132-134	Isaiah 65	Matthew 13
July 4	Joshua 6	Psalms 135-136	Isaiah 66	Matthew 14
July 5	Joshua 7	Psalms 137-138	Jeremiah 1	Matthew 15
July 6	Joshua 8	Psalms 139	Jeremiah 2	Matthew 16
July 7	Joshua 9	Psalms 140-141	Jeremiah 3	Matthew 17
July 8	Joshua 10	Psalms 142-143	Jeremiah 4	Matthew 18
July 9	Joshua 11	Psalms 144	Jeremiah 5	Matthew 19
July 10	Joshua 12-13	Psalms 145	Jeremiah 6	Matthew 20
July 11	Joshua 14-15	Psalms 146-147	Jeremiah 7	Matthew 21
July 12	Joshua 16-17	Psalms 148	Jeremiah 8	Matthew 22
July 13	Joshua 18-19	Psalms 149-150	Jeremiah 9	Matthew 23
July 14	Joshua 20-21	Acts 1	Jeremiah 10	Matthew 24
July 15	Joshua 22	Acts 2	Jeremiah 11	Matthew 25
July 16	Joshua 23	Acts 3	Jeremiah 12	Matthew 26
July 17	Joshua 24	Acts 4	Jeremiah 13	Matthew 27
July 18	Judges 1	Acts 5	Jeremiah 14	Matthew 28
July 19	Judges 2	Acts 6	Jeremiah 15	Mark 1
July 20	Judges 3	Acts 7	Jeremiah 16	Mark 2
July 21	Judges 4	Acts 8	Jeremiah 17	Mark 3
July 22	Judges 5	Acts 9	Jeremiah 18	Mark 4
July 23	Judges 6	Acts 10	Jeremiah 19	Mark 5

July 24	Judges 7	Acts 11	Jeremiah 20	Mark 6
July 25	Judges 8	Acts 12	Jeremiah 21	Mark 7
July 26	Judges 9	Acts 13	Jeremiah 22	Mark 8
July 27	Judges 10	Acts 14	Jeremiah 23	Mark 9
July 28	Judges 11	Acts 15	Jeremiah 24	Mark 10
July 29	Judges 12	Acts 16	Jeremiah 25	Mark 11
July 30	Judges 13	Acts 17	Jeremiah 26	Mark 12
July 31	Judges 14	Acts 18	Jeremiah 27	Mark 13
August 1	Judges 15	Acts 19	Jeremiah 28	Mark 14
August 2	Judges 16	Acts 20	Jeremiah 29	Mark 15
August 3	Judges 17	Acts 21	Jeremiah 30-31	Mark 16
August 4	Judges 18	Acts 22	Jeremiah 32	Psalms 1-2
August 5	Judges 19	Acts 23	Jeremiah 33	Psalms 3-4
August 6	Judges 20	Acts 24	Jeremiah 34	Psalms 5-6
August 7	Judges 21	Acts 25	Jeremiah 35	Psalms 7-8
August 8	Ruth 1	Acts 26	Jeremiah 36, 45	Psalms 9
August 9	Ruth 2	Acts 27	Jeremiah 37	Psalms 10
August 10	Ruth 3-4	Acts 28	Jeremiah 38	Psalms 11-12
August 11	1 Samuel 1	Romans 1	Jeremiah 39	Psalms 13-14
August 12	1 Samuel 2	Romans 2	Jeremiah 40	Psalms 15-16
August 13	1 Samuel 3	Romans 3	Jeremiah 41	Psalms 17
August 14	1 Samuel 4	Romans 4	Jeremiah 42	Psalms 18
August 15	1 Samuel 5-6	Romans 5	Jeremiah 43	Psalms 19
August 16	1 Samuel 7-8	Romans 6	Jeremiah 44	Psalms 20-21
August 17	1 Samuel 9	Romans 7	Jeremiah 46	Psalms 22
August 18	1 Samuel 10	Romans 8	Jeremiah 47	Psalms 23-24
August 19	1 Samuel 11	Romans 9	Jeremiah 48	Psalms 25
August 20	1 Samuel 12	Romans 10	Jeremiah 49	Psalms 26-27
August 21	1 Samuel 13	Romans 11	Jeremiah 50	Psalms 28-29
August 22	1 Samuel 14	Romans 12	Jeremiah 51	Psalms 30
August 23	1 Samuel 15	Romans 13	Jeremiah 52	Psalms 31
August 24	1 Samuel 16	Romans 14	Lamentations 1	Psalms 32
August 25	1 Samuel 17	Romans 15	Lamentations 2	Psalms 33
August 26	1 Samuel 18	Romans 16	Lamentations 3	Psalms 34
August 27	1 Samuel 19	1 Corinthians 1	Lamentations 4	Psalms 35
August 28	1 Samuel 20	1 Corinthians 2	Lamentations 5	Psalms 36
August 29	1 Samuel 21-22	1 Corinthians 3	Ezekiel 1	Psalms 37

August 30	1 Samuel 23	1 Corinthians 4	Ezekiel 2	Psalms 38
August 31	1 Samuel 24	1 Corinthians 5	Ezekiel 3	Psalms 39
September 1	1 Samuel 25	1 Corinthians 6	Ezekiel 4	Psalms 40-41
September 2	1 Samuel 26	1 Corinthians 7	Ezekiel 5	Psalms 42-43
September 3	1 Samuel 27	1 Corinthians 8	Ezekiel 6	Psalms 44
September 4	1 Samuel 28	1 Corinthians 9	Ezekiel 7	Psalms 45
September 5	1 Samuel 29-30	1 Corinthians 10	Ezekiel 8	Psalms 46-47
September 6	1 Samuel 31	1 Corinthians 11	Ezekiel 9	Psalms 48
September 7	2 Samuel 1	1 Corinthians 12	Ezekiel 10	Psalms 49
September 8	2 Samuel 2	1 Corinthians 13	Ezekiel 11	Psalms 50
September 9	2 Samuel 3	1 Corinthians 14	Ezekiel 12	Psalms 51
September 10	2 Samuel 4-5	1 Corinthians 15	Ezekiel 13	Psalms 52-54
September 11	2 Samuel 6	1 Corinthians 16	Ezekiel 14	Psalms 55
September 12	2 Samuel 7	2 Corinthians 1	Ezekiel 15	Psalms 56-57
September 13	2 Samuel 8-9	2 Corinthians 2	Ezekiel 16	Psalms 58-59
September 14	2 Samuel 10	2 Corinthians 3	Ezekiel 17	Psalms 60-61
September 15	2 Samuel 11	2 Corinthians 4	Ezekiel 18	Psalms 62-63
September 16	2 Samuel 12	2 Corinthians 5	Ezekiel 19	Psalms 64-65
September 17	2 Samuel 13	2 Corinthians 6	Ezekiel 20	Psalms 66-67
September 18	2 Samuel 14	2 Corinthians 7	Ezekiel 21	Psalms 68
September 19	2 Samuel 15	2 Corinthians 8	Ezekiel 22	Psalms 69
September 20	2 Samuel 16	2 Corinthians 9	Ezekiel 23	Psalms 70-71
September 21	2 Samuel 17	2 Corinthians 10	Ezekiel 24	Psalms 72
September 22	2 Samuel 18	2 Corinthians 11	Ezekiel 25	Psalms 73
September 23	2 Samuel 19	2 Corinthians 12	Ezekiel 26	Psalms 74
September 24	2 Samuel 20	2 Corinthians 13	Ezekiel 27	Psalms 75-76
September 25	2 Samuel 21	Galatians 1	Ezekiel 28	Psalms 77
September 26	2 Samuel 22	Galatians 2	Ezekiel 29	Psalms 78:1-39
September 27	2 Samuel 23	Galatians 3	Ezekiel 30	Psalms 78:40-72
September 28	2 Samuel 24	Galatians 4	Ezekiel 31	Psalms 79
September 29	1 Kings 1	Galatians 5	Ezekiel 32	Psalms 80
September 30	1 Kings 2	Galatians 6	Ezekiel 33	Psalms 81-82
October 1	1 Kings 3	Ephesians 1	Ezekiel 34	Psalms 83-84
October 2	1 Kings 4-5	Ephesians 2	Ezekiel 35	Psalms 85
October 3	1 Kings 6	Ephesians 3	Ezekiel 36	Psalms 86
October 4	1 Kings 7	Ephesians 4	Ezekiel 37	Psalms 87-88
October 5	1 Kings 8	Ephesians 5	Ezekiel 38	Psalms 89

October 6	1 Kings 9	Ephesians 6	Ezekiel 39	Psalms 90
October 7	1 Kings 10	Philippians 1	Ezekiel 40	Psalms 91
October 8	1 Kings 11	Philippians 2	Ezekiel 41	Psalms 92-93
October 9	1 Kings 12	Philippians 3	Ezekiel 42	Psalms 94
October 10	1 Kings 13	Philippians 4	Ezekiel 43	Psalms 95-96
October 11	1 Kings 14	Colossians 1	Ezekiel 44	Psalms 97-98
October 12	1 Kings 15	Colossians 2	Ezekiel 45	Psalms 99-101
October 13	1 Kings 16	Colossians 3	Ezekiel 46	Psalms 102
October 14	1 Kings 17	Colossians 4	Ezekiel 47	Psalms 103
October 15	1 Kings 18	1 Thessalonians 1	Ezekiel 48	Psalms 104
October 16	1 Kings 19	1 Thessalonians 2	Daniel 1	Psalms 105
October 17	1 Kings 20	1 Thessalonians 3	Daniel 2	Psalms 106
October 18	1 Kings 21	1 Thessalonians 4	Daniel 3	Psalms 107
October 19	1 Kings 22	1 Thessalonians 5	Daniel 4	Psalms 108-109
October 20	2 Kings 1	2 Thessalonians 1	Daniel 5	Psalms 110-111
October 21	2 Kings 2	2 Thessalonians 2	Daniel 6	Psalms 112-113
October 22	2 Kings 3	2 Thessalonians 3	Daniel 7	Psalms 114-115
October 23	2 Kings 4	1 Timothy 1	Daniel 8	Psalms 116
October 24	2 Kings 5	1 Timothy 2	Daniel 9	Psalms 117-118
October 25	2 Kings 6	1 Timothy 3	Daniel 10	Psalms 119:1-24
October 26	2 Kings 7	1 Timothy 4	Daniel 11	Psalms 119:25-48
October 27	2 Kings 8	1 Timothy 5	Daniel 12	Psalms 119:49-72
October 28	2 Kings 9	1 Timothy 6	Hosea 1	Psalms 119:73-96
October 29	2 Kings 10-11	2 Timothy 1	Hosea 2	Psalms 119:97-120
October 30	2 Kings 12	2 Timothy 2	Hosea 3-4	Psalms 119:121-144
October 31	2 Kings 13	2 Timothy 3	Hosea 5-6	Psalms 119:145-176
November 1	2 Kings 14	2 Timothy 4	Hosea 7	Psalms 120-122
November 2	2 Kings 15	Titus 1	Hosea 8	Psalms 123-125
November 3	2 Kings 16	Titus 2	Hosea 9	Psalms 126-128
November 4	2 Kings 17	Titus 3	Hosea 10	Psalms 129-131
November 5	2 Kings 18	Philemon	Hosea 11	Psalms 132-134
November 6	2 Kings 19	Hebrews 1	Hosea 12	Psalms 135-136
November 7	2 Kings 20	Hebrews 2	Hosea 13	Psalms 137-138
November 8	2 Kings 21	Hebrews 3	Hosea 14	Psalms 139
November 9	2 Kings 22	Hebrews 4	Joel 1	Psalms 140-141

November 10	2 Kings 23	Hebrews 5	Joel 2	Psalms 142-143
November 11	2 Kings 24	Hebrews 6	Joel 3	Psalms 144
November 12	2 Kings 25	Hebrews 7	Amos 1	Psalms 145
November 13	1 Chronicles 1-2	Hebrews 8	Amos 2	Psalms 146-147
November 14	1 Chronicles 3-4	Hebrews 9	Amos 3	Psalms 148
November 15	1 Chronicles 5-6	Hebrews 10	Amos 4	Psalms 149-150
November 16	1 Chronicles 7-8	Hebrews 11	Amos 5	Luke 1:1-38
November 17	1 Chronicles 9-10	Hebrews 12	Amos 6	Luke 1:39-80
November 18	1 Chronicles 11-12	Hebrews 13	Amos 7	Luke 2
November 19	1 Chronicles 13-14	James 1	Amos 8	Luke 3
November 20	1 Chronicles 15	James 2	Amos 9	Luke 4
November 21	1 Chronicles 16	James 3	Obadiah	Luke 5
November 22	1 Chronicles 17	James 4	Jonah 1	Luke 6
November 23	1 Chronicles 18	James 5	Jonah 2	Luke 7
November 24	1 Chronicles 19-20	1 Peter 1	Jonah 3	Luke 8
November 25	1 Chronicles 21	1 Peter 2	Jonah 4	Luke 9
November 26	1 Chronicles 22	1 Peter 3	Micah 1	Luke 10
November 27	1 Chronicles 23	1 Peter 4	Micah 2	Luke 11
November 28	1 Chronicles 24-25	1 Peter 5	Micah 3	Luke 12
November 29	1 Chronicles 26-27	2 Peter 1	Micah 4	Luke 13
November 30	1 Chronicles 28	2 Peter 2	Micah 5	Luke 14
December 1	1 Chronicles 29	2 Peter 3	Micah 6	Luke 15
December 2	2 Chronicles 1	1 John 1	Micah 7	Luke 16
December 3	2 Chronicles 2	1 John 2	Nahum 1	Luke 17
December 4	2 Chronicles 3-4	1 John 3	Nahum 2	Luke 18
December 5	2 Chronicles 5:1-6:11	1 John 4	Nahum 3	Luke 19
December 6	2 Chronicles 6:12-42	1 John 5	Habakkuk 1	Luke 20
December 7	2 Chronicles 7	2 John	Habakkuk 2	Luke 21
December 8	2 Chronicles 8	3 John	Habakkuk 3	Luke 22
December 9	2 Chronicles 9	Jude	Zephaniah 1	Luke 23
December 10	2 Chronicles 10	Revelation 1	Zephaniah 2	Luke 24
December 11	2 Chronicles 11-12	Revelation 2	Zephaniah 3	John 1
December 12	2 Chronicles 13	Revelation 3	Haggai 1	John 2
December 13	2 Chronicles 14-15	Revelation 4	Haggai 2	John 3
December 14	2 Chronicles 16	Revelation 5	Zechariah 1	John 4

December 15	2 Chronicles 17	Revelation 6	Zechariah 2	John 5
December 16	2 Chronicles 18	Revelation 7	Zechariah 3	John 6
December 17	2 Chronicles 19-20	Revelation 8	Zechariah 4	John 7
December 18	2 Chronicles 21	Revelation 9	Zechariah 5	John 8
December 19	2 Chronicles 22-23	Revelation 10	Zechariah 6	John 9
December 20	2 Chronicles 24	Revelation 11	Zechariah 7	John 10
December 21	2 Chronicles 25	Revelation 12	Zechariah 8	John 11
December 22	2 Chronicles 26	Revelation 13	Zechariah 9	John 12
December 23	2 Chronicles 27-28	Revelation 14	Zechariah 10	John 13
December 24	2 Chronicles 29	Revelation 15	Zechariah 11	John 14
December 25	2 Chronicles 30	Revelation 16	Zechariah 12	John 15
December 26	2 Chronicles 31	Revelation 17	Zechariah 13	John 16
December 27	2 Chronicles 32	Revelation 18	Zechariah 14	John 17
December 28	2 Chronicles 33	Revelation 19	Malachi 1	John 18
December 29	2 Chronicles 34	Revelation 20	Malachi 2	John 19
December 30	2 Chronicles 35	Revelation 21	Malachi 3	John 20
December 31	2 Chronicles 36	Revelation 22	Malachi 4	John 21

NOTES

1 Thomas G. Long, "No News is Bad News" in Mike Graves, ed., *What's the Matter with Preaching Today?* (Louisville: Westminster John Knox, 2004), 146–147.

2 C. E. B. Cranfield, *The First Epistle of Peter* (London: SCM, 1950), 32.

3 M. A. C. Warren, *Crowded Canvas* (London: Hodder & Stoughton, 1974), 143.

4 Article 20 of the Thirty-Nine Articles of the Church of England.

5 Leland Ryken, "The Bible as Literature and Expository Preaching" in Leland Ryken and Todd Wilson, eds., *Preach the Word: Essays on Expository Preaching in Honor of R. Kent Hughes* (Wheaton: Crossway, 2007), 50.

6 Leland Ryken, "The Bible as Literature and Expository Preaching" in Ryken and Wilson, *Preach the Word*, 44.

7 Alexander Solzhenitsyn, *One Word of Truth*, the 1970 Nobel Speech on Literature (Bodley Head, 1972; Farrer, Strausz & Giroux, 1970), 22.

8 P. T. Forsyth, *Positive Preaching and the Modern Mind* (1907; repr. Whitefish, Mont: Kessinger, 2003), 3.

9 C. H. Spurgeon, *All-Round Ministry* (1900; Edinburgh: Banner of Truth, 1960), 187.

10 D. Martyn Lloyd-Jones, *Preaching and Preachers* (Hodder & Stoughton, 1971), 24.

11 Philip Graham Ryken, *City on a Hill: Reclaiming the Biblical Pattern for the Church in the 21st Century* (Chicago: Moody, 2003), 48–49.

12 David A. Hubbard, "Some Musings on the Preacher's Task". Unpublished paper quoted in Michael P. Halcomb, "The Use of Metaphor in Preaching" (D. Min. thesis presented to Bethel Theological Seminary, 1982), 119.

13 Jean Cadier, *The Man God Mastered: A Brief Biography of John Calvin*

(trans. O. R. Johnston; Inter-Varsity Fellowship, 1960), 173–175.

14 John Bright, *The Authority of the Old Testament* (Grand Rapids: Baker, 1975), 168–169.

15 Adapted from Bauer, Arndt and Gingrich, *A Greek–English Lexicon of the New Testament and Other Early Christian Literature.* The same verb is used in Proverbs 3:6 and 11:5.

16 Charles Silvester Horne, *The Romance of Preaching,* the 1914 Yale Lectures (New York: Fleming H. Revell, 1914), 135, 144–145.

17 S. E. Dwight, *The Works of President Edwards* (New York: Carvill, 1830), 1:606.

18 Arthur Michael Ramsey and Leon-Joseph Suenens, *The Future of the Christian Church* (London: S.C.M., 1971), 13, 14. See also C. H. Spurgeon's tract, "The Bible and the Newspaper", *Lectures to My Students.* Third Series. (London: Passmore and Alabaster, 1894; repr. Grand Rapids: Zondervan, 1980), 54.

19 Ian Pitt-Watson, *A Kind of Folly: Towards a Practical Theology of Preaching,* The 1972–75 Warrack Lectures (Edinburgh: St Andrew Press, 1976), 57.

20 S. C. Neill, *On the Ministry* (London: S.C.M., 1952), 74.

21 For more about these subjects, see John Stott, *Major Issues for a New Century: Vol. 1: Human Rights and Human Wrongs; Vol. 2: Our Social and Sexual Revolution* (Grand Rapids: Baker, 1999).

22 Spurgeon, *All-Round Ministry,* 236.

23 Phillips Brooks, *The Joy of Preaching* (1877, with the title *Lectures on Preaching;* repr. Grand Rapids, Kregel, 1989), 159–160.

24 Two companion books by D. A. Carson help readers by underscoring important lessons from the various chapters, *For the Love of God: A Daily Companion for Discovering the Riches of God's Word* (2 vols.; Wheaton: Crossway, 2006).

25 *The Willowbank Report on Gospel and Culture* (Lausanne Occasional Paper No. 2, 1978), 11. Available at www.lausanne.org/all-documents/lop-2.html.

26 These words are reputed to have been spoken by John Robinson, the pastor of the church in Holland from which the Pilgrim Fathers sailed to America in the *Mayflower* in 1620.

27 Two books that can help you choose commentaries are Tremper Longman, III, *Old Testament Commentary Survey,* 4th ed. and D. A. Carson, *New Testament Commentary Survey,* 6th ed. Both books were published in Grand Rapids by Baker in 2007.

28 Tokunboh Adeyemo (ed.), *Africa Bible Commentary* (Nairobi: WordAlive /

Grand Rapids, Zondervan, 2006).

29 Michael Hennell, *John Venn and the Clapham Sect* (Lutherworth, 1958), 84. In 1955, having recognized our generation's need for "mutual religious intercourse ... and the investigation of spiritual truth", an invitation went out from All Souls Church, Langham Place, to twenty-two younger evangelical ministers to re-found this society. By 1966 it had a membership of over 1,000 in seventeen groups.

30 Warren Wiersbe, *Walking with the Giants: A Minister's Guide to Good Reading and Great Preaching* (Grand Rapids: Baker, 1976), 56.

31 Wiersbe, *Walking with the Giants,* 133.

32 Lloyd-Jones, *Preaching,* 173.

33 James S. Stewart, *Heralds of God* (London: Hodder & Stoughton, 1946), 111.

34 James Stalker, *The Preacher and his Models.* The 1891 Yale Lectures on Preaching (London: Hodder & Stoughton, 1891), 166.

35 Mary Bosanquet, *The Life and Death of Dietrich Bonhoeffer* (London: Hodder & Stoughton, 1968), 110.

36 E. D. Hirsch, *Validity in Interpretation* (New Haven: Yale University Press, 1967), 1.

37 Pitt-Watson, *A Kind of Folly,* 65.

38 Hugh Evan Hopkins, *Charles Simeon of Cambridge* (London: Hodder & Stoughton, 1977), 59.

39 Smyth, *The Art of Preaching,* 177.

40 W. Robertson Nicoll, *Princes of the Church* (London: Hodder & Stoughton, 1921), 245, 249.

41 Spurgeon, *Lectures to My Students,* First Series, 88–89.

42 W. H. Lewis, ed., *Letters of C. S. Lewis* (Geoffrey Bles, 1966), 271.

43 J. C. Ryle, *Light from Old Times* (London: Thynne & Jarvis, 1924), 408.

44 Henry Ward Beecher, *Lectures on Preaching: Personal Elements in Preaching,* the 1872 Yale Lectures (London: Nelson, 1872), 127, 134.

45 Theodore Parker Ferris, *Go Tell the People,* the 1950 George Craig Stewart Lectures on Preaching (New York: Scribner, 1951), 93.

46 Richard Bernard, *The Faithfull Shepheard* (London, 1607), 11, 72. See also William Perkins's *The Art of Prophecying* (London, 1631), in which chapter 7 is entitled "Of the wayes how to use and apply doctrines'. He lists different groups of people and how to relate our message to them.

47 Edwin Charles Dargan, *A History of Preaching* (London: Hodder & Stoughton, 1912), 2:314–315.

48 This sermon was preached in All Souls Church, Langham Place, by Roger Simpson.

49 Smyth, *The Art*, 178.

50 Dwight, *The Works of President Edwards*, 1:605.

51 E. Clowes Chorley, *Men and Movements in the American Episcopal Church*, the Hale Lectures (New York: Scribner, 1946), 34–35.

52 From a private communication dated 30 September 1978.

53 Baxter, *Reformed Pastor*, 158.

54 Halford Edward Luccock, *In the Minister's Workshop* (New York: Abingdon-Cokesbury Press, 1944), 12.

55 Baxter, *Reformed Pastor*, 162.

56 Spurgeon, *Lectures to My Students*, First Series, 4.

57 W. Haslam, *From Death into Life* (London: Marshall, Morgan & Scott, 1880), 48–49.

58 J. H. Bavinck, *An Introduction to the Science of Missions* (Philadelphia: Presbyterian and Reformed, 1960), 93.

59 James Black, *The Mystery of Preaching* (1924; rev. ed.; London: Marshall, Morgan & Scott, 1977).

60 Colin Morris, *The Word and the Words* (London: Epworth, 1975), 34, 35.

61 One of these friends was Tony Waterson, who became Professor of Virology at the Royal Post-graduate Medical School, Hammersmith. He is modest enough to say that, on reflection, his comments were "probably brash, ill-considered and immature", and that they concerned technicalities of structure and delivery rather than the really important questions of whether God was anointing the message, Jesus was being exalted, and people were being blessed. But I think he underestimates the help and challenge he gave me.

62 James W. Alexander, *Thoughts on Preaching* (1864; Edinburgh: Banner of Truth, 1975), 20.

63 John A. Broadus, *On the Preparation and Delivery of Sermons* (1870; rev. ed.; New York: Harper, 1944), 218.

64 David Smith on 2 John 12 in the *Expositor's Greek Testament*.

65 Pollock, *George Whitefield*, 263.

66 Spurgeon, *Lectures to My Students*, Second Series, 46.

67 Alexander, *Thoughts on Preaching*, 25.

68 G. C. Morgan, *Preaching* (1937; repr. Grand Rapids: Baker, 1974), 14, 15.

69 G. C. Morgan, *Preaching*, 36.

70 Lloyd-Jones, *Preaching*, 97.

71 T. R. Glover, *The Jesus of History* (1917; Hodder & Stoughton, 1965), 44.

72 Elton Trueblood, *The Humour of Christ* (Harper & Row, 1964; Darton, Longman & Todd, 1965), 49–53.

73 Josephine Kamm, *Men Who Served Africa* (London: Harrap, 1957), 154.

74 Christopher Morley, quoted in Luccock, *In the Minister's Workshop*, 192.

75 E. M. Bounds, *Power Through Prayer* (London: Marshall, Morgan & Scott, 1912), 11. See also Al Martin, *What's Wrong with Preaching Today?* (Edinburgh: Banner of Truth, 1968).

76 James Black, *The Mystery of Preaching,* the 1923 Warrack and Sprunt Lectures (1924; rev. ed. Marshall, Morgan & Scott, 1977), 37.

77 George Buttrick, *Jesus Came Preaching: Christian Preaching in the New Age,* the 1931 Yale lectures (New York: Scribner, 1931), 133.

78 Dargan, *A History of Preaching*, 1:90.

79 Luther, *Works*, 21:201–202.

80 Elizabeth Whitley, *Plain Mr Knox* (Scottish Reformation Society, 1960), 199, 235.

81 Coretta Scott King, *My Life with Martin Luther King, Jr* (New York: Holt, Rinehart, and Winston, 1969), 18.

82 Nicoll, *Princes*, 320.

83 Chad Walsh, *Campus Gods on Trial* (New York: Macmillan, 1962), 95.

84 John C. Pollock, *Amazing Grace* (Hodder & Stoughton, 1981), 155.

85 Forsyth, *Positive Preaching,* 5

86 Forsyth, *Positive Preaching,* 19.

87 Beecher, *Popular Lectures*, 249, referring to the incident recorded in Dan 4:28–37.

88 Baxter, *Reformed Pastor*, 95.

89 Ralph G. Turnbull, *A Minister's Obstacles* (1946; Grand Rapids: Baker, 1972), 41.

90 Donald G. Miller, *Fire in Thy Mouth* (Nashville: Abingdon, 1954), 18.

91 J. H. Jowett, *The Preacher: His Life and Work,* the 1912 Yale Lectures (New York: G. H. Doran, 1912), 24.

92 *Didache* 11:1–2; 12:1–5 (www.earlychristianwritings.com/text/didache-roberts.html).

93 *Didache*, 3:8; 4:1.

94 Justin Martyr, "Weekly Worship of the Christians" in *First Apology,* lxvii (www.earlychristianwritings.com/text/justinmartyr-firstapology.html).

95 Tertullian, *Apology*, xxxix (www.earlychristianwritings.com/text/tertul-

lian01.html).

96 Philip Schaff (ed.), *The Nicene and Post-Nicene Fathers* (1892; Eerdmans 1975), 9:22. (www.ccel.org/ccel/schaff/npnf109.iii.xiv.html).

97 Clyde E. Fant and William M. Pinson, eds., *Twenty Centuries of Great Preaching* (Waco: Word, 1971), 1:108–109.

98 Fant and Pinson, *Twenty Centuries*, 1:174–175.

99 Charles Smyth, *The Art of Preaching: A Practical Survey of Preaching in the Church of England* (London: SPCK, 1940), 15–16.

100 "De Blasphemia contra Fratres", in Fant and Pinson, *Twenty Centuries*, 1:234.

101 Erasmus, "On Preaching", in Roland H. Bainton, *Erasmus of Christendom* (London: Collins, 1970), 324.

102 Martin Luther, "A Prelude on the Babylonian Captivity of the Church", in Ernest Gordon Rupp, *Luther's Progress to the Diet of Worms 1521* (London: SCM, 1951), 85–86.

103 Luther, "Of the Liberty of a Christian Man", in Rupp, *Luther's Progress*, 87.

104 Luther, "Treatise on Good Works", in Helmut T. Lehmann, *Luther's Works* (Minneapolis: Fortress, 1965), 44:58.

105 "Of Preachers and Preaching", in *Luther's Table-Talk*, 1566 (Captain Henry Bell, 1886), cccc.

106 Rupp, *Luther's Progress*, 96–99.

107 Richard Baxter, *The Reformed Pastor* (1656; London: Epworth, 1950), 75.

108 Baxter, *Reformed Pastor*, 81.

109 Cotton Mather, *Student and Preacher, or Directions for a Candidate of the Ministry* (1726; London: Hindmarsh, 1789), iii–v.

110 John Wesley, *Sermons on Several Occasions* (1746–60; London: Epworth, 1944), vi.

111 John C. Pollock, *George Whitefield and the Great Awakening* (London: Hodder & Stoughton, 1973), 248.

112 William Carus, ed., *Memoirs of the Rev. Charles Simeon* (London: Hatchard, 1847), 41.

113 Charles Simeon, *Let Wisdom Judge: University Addresses and Sermon Outlines* (ed. Arthur Pollard: London: Inter-Varsity Fellowship, 1959), 188–189.

114 Herman Melville, *Moby Dick* (1851; Penguin, 1972), 128–242.

115 Hughes Oliphant Old, *The Reading and Preaching of the Scriptures in the Worship of the Christian Church* (Grand Rapids: Eerdmans, 1998–2007),

6:826–829.

[116] Old, *Reading and Preaching*, 6:835.

[117] James S. Stewart, "Heralds of God", the 1946 Warrack Lectures, as reported in Old, *Reading and Preaching*, 6:908.

[118] Old, *Reading and Preaching*, 6:904.

[119] Walter M. Abbott, ed., *The Documents of Vatican II* (London: Geoffrey Chapman, 1967), para. 23.

[120] D. Martyn Lloyd-Jones, *Preaching and Preachers* (London, Hodder & Stoughton, 1971), 9, 297.

FURTHER READING

Adam, Peter, *Speaking God's Words: A Practical Theology of Expository Preaching*. Downers Grove: InterVarsity Press, 1996.

Green, Christopher and David Jackman (eds), *When God's Voice is Heard: The Power of Preaching*. Leicester: IVP, 2003.

Johnson, Darrell W., *The Glory of Preaching: Participating in God's Transformation of the World*. Downers Grove: IVP Academic, 2009.

Robinson, Haddon W., *Biblical Preaching*, 2nd ed. Grand Rapids: Baker Academic, 2001.

Scharf, Greg, *Prepared to Preach: God's Work and Ours in Proclaiming His Word*. Fearn, Scotland: Christian Focus, 2005.

Wright, Christopher J. H. and Jonathan Lamb, *Understanding and Using the Bible*, London: SPCK, 2009.

OTHER PUBLICATIONS FROM LANGHAM PREACHING RESOURCES

Relational Preaching by Greg Scharf (2010)
Available in Paperback & Ebook

Prêcher La Grande Histoire De Dieu by Phil Crowter (2012)
Available in Paperback

Forthcoming

The Dynamics of Preaching by Jonathan Lamb
Preaching from the Old Testament by Christopher J.H. Wright
Knowing Jesus Through the Old Testament by Christopher J.H. Wright